A Funny Thing Happened

On My Way to the Retirement Home!!

(Ageless Humor with Some Inspirational Thoughts, Too)

For those over 55 and do not have a computer.

Compiled by

Glen Wheeler

Koinonia Associates
Knoxville, Tennessee

ISBN 978-1-60658-023-3

Published by:
Koinonia Associates
7809 Timber Glow Trail
Knoxville, TN 37938

To learn how you can become a published author,
visit PublishwithKA.com
November 18, 2011

Cover Photo – Courtyard of the Worthington Christian Village, Columbus, OH.
Photographer – Erin Hodge, Columbus, OH
Cover Design – Sarah Wells, Columbus, OH

Table of Contents

GREETINGS

Frequently people have said, "You ought to write a book of your stories." Well, here it is so smile along with me.

Collecting quotes, one liners, humorous stories, etc. has been an aspect of my ministry. Having lived at in a retirement village for over 20 years, the residents have provided an endless supply of Senior Citizens stories.

Most seniors hesitate to learn using a computer and others because of health issues are unable to use one, thus they miss the source of many emails. I have combined my personal collection of humorous Seniors stories with several from e-mails.

Most humorous stories do not give an author or the source from which it was taken. This prevents giving credits in the book. Stories also have variations which makes determining which is the original version almost impossible. I have given credit where known. Inform me if you know the author of a story and it will be acknowledged in future editions.

As you read these efforts, might your prayer be:

Give me a sense of humor, Lord,
Give me the grace to see a joke,
To get some humor out of life,
And pass it on to other folk.

--Glen Wheeler, *Compiler*

A cheerful heart brings good healing, but a crushed spirit dries up the bones. (Pro 17:22)

Laughter is an instant vacation.
--Milton Berle

A joyful heart makes the face cheerful...and the cheerful heart a continual feast.
(Prov. 15:13,15)

Grow old along with me! The best is yet to be. The last of life for which the first was made.
--Robert Browning

A DAY WITHOUT LAUGHTER IS A DAY WASTED!!!

A man isn't poor if he can still laugh.

A PERSONAL MESSAGE TO THE READER

Perhaps the most difficult decision Seniors face, is selling their home and moving to a condo, in with one of the children, or selecting a retirement center.

Health, the many tasks of keeping up “the home place”, a desire to be closer to the children and grandchildren or other factors make such a decision necessary.

It is an emotional experience, especially if one has lived in the same house for many years, or if it was THE dream house, you and your spouse built it with your own hands, or if a move of many miles is required. Parting with familiar furniture, family antiques, and personal treasures, increase the emotions about a move. Age does not welcome change easily.

Far too many believe that moving to a retirement center is in indication their days are numbered. Changing doctors, making new friends, leaving life long friends, changing churches, and adjusting to congregate living can easily bring tears and heartaches as well as fear of the unknown.

And then a preacher has the audacity to compile a book of humor about moving to a retirement center!! With all of the above emotions, why would anyone want to laugh? Certainly for most that is not a happy time.

But it can be! Since 1989. I have lived at the Worthington Christian Village in Columbus, OH. For twelve years I served as chaplain. People move here to LIVE, not to DIE, and we have a great life together. It is a great way to live, retire, and enjoy "maturity."

Tons of funny things happen at a retirement center. Seniors have more things to laugh about than any other age group. We have lived longer and "been there and done that."

Smile, even laugh out loud, and share with your friends these stories and quotes from more than 65 years of ministry. It will do you good mentally, physically and spiritually.

Remember, every one needs to have a deep belly laugh every day. If men do not have one, their hair falls out. If women do not have one, their hips spread. Smile—people will wonder what you are up to!

Enjoy the book. Read it often. Buy copies for your friends for if you loan your copy, the borrower will forget to whom it belongs.

This is the day that the Lord has made, we will rejoice....!!!

Glen Wheeler, *Compiler*

BLESSED ARE THEY

who can laugh at themselves for they shall never cease to be entertained.

– Anonymous

PERSONALLY FROM THE COMPILER

I am aware that some people do not have a sense of humor and others consider humor a form of ridicule or a hidden insult.

All of the stories in this book are intended to bring a smile to your face, to lift a burden you may be carrying, or to help turn the tears you shed, into a joyous heart.

Never would I intentionally offend anyone through humor, spoken or written so do not read any of these stories with that attitude in mind.

The Bible never uses smile in the KJV, however laugh, happy, content, are found. Rejoice is used 192 times. So the Christian can rejoice, can sing, can laugh and be victorious even in the storms of life. We are to do more than smile.

Some of these stories are over 60 years old, others you may have heard several times, some are short, others long (like sermons), but all can be shared without embarrassment.

Laugh often, long and loud. Laugh until you gasp for breath. And if you have a friend who makes you laugh, spend lots and lots of time with them.

MY FAVORITE SENIOR CITIZEN STORY

TWO ELDERLY LADIES STREAKING

It was Sunday afternoon in the Nursing Center. Susie and Sarah were lonesome and bored. They discussed what they could do to bring some life and enthusiasm into the facility. Susie said, "Sarah, let's streak."

At the end of the hall they disrobed and with their walkers, slowly proceeded down the hall.

They passed the room where Bill and Joe sat, tied to their geriatric chairs and Bill said, "Joe, did you see that?" Bill said, "Yes, Joe. What were they wearing?" And Joe replied, "I don't know, but it needed ironing."

MY FAVORITE SENIOR CITIZEN STORY # 2

THE GOWN THAT IS SPLIT DOWN THE BACK

I was sittin' here mindin' my business,
Kinda lettin' my mind go slack,
When in comes a nurse with a bright, sunny smile,
And a gown that was split down the back.

"Take a shower," she said, "and get ready,
And then jump into this sack."
What she was really talkin' about
Was the gown with the split down the back.

"They're coming to do some tests," she said.
They're gonna stretch me out on a rack,
With nothin' twixt me and the cold, cruel world,
But that gown that's split down the back!

It comes only to the knees in front,
In the sides there is also a lack,
But by far the greatest shortcoming
Is that bloomin' split down the back.

Whoever designed this garment,
For humor had a great knack.

But I fail to see anything funny
'Bout a gown that's split down the back.

I hear them coming to get me,
The wheels going clickety-clack.
I'll ride through the halls on a table,
In a gown with a split down the back!

When I get to Heaven it'll make me no odds
If my robe is white, red, or black.
The only thing I will ask is, "Please, Lord,
Give me one with no split down the back."

Habit: A habit is something you have---and then it has you.

The shortest distance between two points is under construction.

Ambidextrous means being clumsy with both hands.

Show me a man with both feet on the ground and I'll show you a men who can't get his pants on.

A SENIOR CITIZEN'S LAMENT

Thought I'd let my doctor check me
'Cause I didn't feel quite right.
All those aches and pains annoyed me
And I couldn't sleep at night.

He could find no real disorder
But he wouldn't let it rest.
Why with Medicare and Blue Cross
It wouldn't hurt to do some tests.

To the hospital he sent me
Though I didn't feel that bad.
He arranged for them to give me
Every test that could be had.

I was fluoroscope and cystoscoped,
My aging frame displayed
Strapped upon an ice cold table
While my gizzards were x-rayed.

I was checked for worms and parasites
For fungus and the crud
While they shoved long needles in me
Taking samples of my blood.

Doctors came to check me over
Probed and pushed and poked around.
And to make sure I was living

Had me wired up for sound.

They have finally concluded;
Their results fill many a page,
What I have will some day kill me--
My affliction is OLD AGE!
-- Copied

A QUICK SOLUTION

A speaker went to great lengths to explain to a large group of elderly citizens the dangers of dealing with telemarketers. The man explained that while many callers are legitimate, there are others who particularly prey on seniors. He described the scam artist's tactics and how to recognize them. He warned the group not to give out Social Security or credit card numbers, to ask for references etc.

Following his long discourse, he asked for questions. A small boy who was with his grandmother raised his hand. Smiling the speaker asked, "What is it, son?"

Innocently the boy asked, "Why didn't you just tell them to hang up?"

The only thing more beautiful than the sight of freshly fallen snow, is the sight of someone shoveling your walk.

BRING ME A SUNDAE

An elderly couple were in their rocking chairs on the porch of their retirement village home. She asked if he would go to the drug store and get her a sundae.

He agreed and then she began giving her wishes. "Bring me one with vanilla ice cream with marshmallow cream on top. Now you had better write it down for you know you easily forget."

"I can remember, vanilla ice cream with marshmallow cream on top," he replied.

"And have them put some sprinkles on it and a cherry on top. Now write it down so you won't forget," she advised.

"I know. Vanilla ice cream, marshmallow cream, sprinkles and a cherry on top," he repeated.

He left and in a few moments he returned and handed her a sandwich. She thanked him, unwrapped it and then in a very disgusted voice she exclaimed, "I knew you should have written it down. I asked you to bring mustard and you brought catsup."

A small child yearns for security, and then,

so does his father, his grandfather and his great-grand father.

WE ARE SISTERS

Two unmarried sisters lived together. They were stingy. So stingy they would not buy anything they did not need. For an example, they only had one set of false teeth between them. If one was invited out, she wore the teeth; the other had to stay at home.

Susie was invited out. Mary stayed home. When Susie returned, Mary pleaded, "Oh, give me the falth teeth. My gums are killin' me." Susie handed them over.

After making sure they were secure, Mary asked, "What did you have to eat." With a lisp, Susie told her. "Masted tatoes. Thewed peas. Thrawberry Thortcake."

With a gesture familiar to Seniors, Mary drew air over and between the false teeth and said, "You had fried chicken, too, didn't you?"

(I told this story over 66 years ago in my first ministry at Harriman, TN. It was never forgotten—and maybe never forgiven!-GVW)

I have been teaching my 3-year- old granddaughter safe street crossing behavior. At each intersection I stoop to her eye level, point, and look both ways before taking her hand and crossing the street. On a recent outing I tested her and was amazed at how closely she had been paying attention.

Stopping at the curb, she pointed and looked each way, then clasped my hand and assured me, "It's O.K. to cross, Gamma"-all from a stooped position.

--Linda Rector Reaves

THE WEDDING

The Bride, white of hair, leans over her cane,
Her footsteps, uncertain, need guiding;
While down the church aisle, with a toothless
smile,
The Groom, in his wheelchair, comes riding.

"Now who is this elderly couple?" you ask.
You'll find if you'll closely explore it,
That here is that rare, most unusual pair.
Who waited till they could afford it!

ALWAYS PROSPECTING

The new chaplain had been on duty at the Retirement Home about four months, when one of the ladies approached him and said, "Chaplain, you look just like my third husband."

His response was, "Thank you, but how many have you had?"

She proudly answered, "Two."

DIPLOMACY

Looking at my wedding album, 5-year-old grandson cried, "Oh, Grandma, you were so beautiful when you were young."

He studied the photo intently then suddenly slapped it.

"Why?" I asked.

Snuggling up to me, he said, "I don't love that pretty girl. I love this sweet lady sitting here beside me!"

--Marie Elledge

A BROKEN ENGAGEMENT

Susie came in from a date and announced to her Mother that she had broken her engagement to Johnny. Surprised, her mother asked, "Why?" Susie said, "Because he does not believe there is a hell."

Her mother replied, "Susie, you go ahead and marry him and between you and me we will prove to him that there is one."

MISUNDERSTOOD

As we grow older, our hearing becomes weaker and we do not always hear things correctly. A couple, sitting on the porch of the retirement home, were enjoying their rocking chairs. The wife tapped her husband on his knee and said, "I admire you", to which he replied, "I'm tired of you, too".

BAD FOUR LETTER WORDS

Mary and Alice were close friends and members of the Senior center. Mary was dating Harry, also a member. At lunch one day, Mary told Alice that she had broken up with Harry because of his use of four letter words. Alice was horrified. "Harry using four letter words! I never would have thought he would use such language." Then she whispered to Mary, "Do you mind telling me what words he used?" Mary said, "Yes. Wash. Dust. Iron. Cook."

Good friends are like stars. You don't always see them, but you know they are always there.

Years ago when men cursed and beat the ground with sticks, it was called witchcraft.

Today, it's called golf.

A SIMPLE SOLUTION

An older couple had one disagreement after another. Their marriage was on shaky ground. Finally they decided to consult a marriage counselor.

They arrived at the office, and after a few moments of pleasantries, the counselor asked, "What problems are you having that caused you to come to me?"

With that opening, the wife began: "He's never home. He never takes me anywhere. He never compliments my cooking. He never helps me with the cleaning. All he wants to do is watch television or play golf. He never gives me any money." She went on with her complaints for a half an hour without stopping.

Finally the counselor said, "I think I know what will help your marriage to be stronger and happier." With that, he arose from his chair, walked over to where the wife was sitting, looked at the husband, and said, "This is all you wife needs" and with that he bent over and hugged and kissed and loved on the wife like she had never been treated in months.

When he stood up, he looked at the husband and said, "There. That's all your wife needs and she needs it at least once a day."

The man thought for a moment and finally

said, "Well, I think I can bring her in on Monday, Wednesday and Friday. But she will have to find a way to get here Tuesday and Thursday herself, for those are the days I play golf."

PRE PLANNING

A 92 year old lady, who had never married, outlined her ideas for her funeral. She then visited the funeral home and discussed the plans with the director. The music, the scriptures, and the bulletins presented no problems.

The director, however, questioned why all of her pallbearers were women because usually men served in that capacity.

The aged lady responded, " I intend for the pallbearers to be women. The men didn't take me out when I was alive and by cracky, they are not going to take me out when I'm dead."

ABOUT WRINKLES

Although the years bring aches and pains
That render our muscles inert,
One consolation still remains--
Thank goodness our wrinkles don't hurt.

CAIN AND ABLE

A senior citizen apartment complex in Florida serves its meals cafeteria-style. They have separate lines--one for those with wheelchairs, walkers, and other aids, and another for diners without handicaps. Residents have dubbed the two lines "Cane" and "Able".

The first thing lost on a diet is one's sense of humor.

--Guy Belleranti

A PRAYER OF THE AGED

"Dear Lord, I sit and dream so very much,
I cannot seem to keep the rapid pace;
I'm just a little weary and am not in touch
With all the hurried movements of the place.
But I can watch, and help some here and there
And mend the little breaks that come my way,
And with your help, Dear Lord, I think I'll fare
Quite well; and thank you for each lovely day.

I thank you for the younger ones who come
and go
And for the good full life that I have had;

The hour glass now runs just a little low.
For memories of those other days I'm glad,
Now, if the tide of life runs by me all too fast,
There's nearly always in that golden stream
Some little back-wash as it rushes past
Some little tiny inlet where I dream;

Some tiny bit of flotsam on life's sea
Some bruised and broken soul who seeketh peace,
And there the little strength thou gavest me
May shelter, and retrieve, and bring release.
My feet are slow, and too, my fumbling hands,
Seem not to seek the busy once-loved task;
My spirit wanders far in brighter lands,
Nor greater joy wants, nor pleasure asks;

Dear Lord, I'm not alone, so long as Thou
Art near me, with a loving outstretched hand;
I only ask you tarry with me now
And journey with me to that brighter better land."

--Mrs. R. E. Walston

THE PRIME OF LIFE

They say at sixty-five I'm old.
Beware of drafts, don't catch a cold.
Look down at every step you take,
Don't trip and fall or bones will break.

Be sure to drink your Metrical
And keep a cat or dog as pal.
Try not to worry or get upset,
You could live to be a hundred yet!

What I really need are kisses sweet
And hugs from every girl I meet.
If age can offer only tears,
Why should I live a hundred years?

So, friends, forget your good advice,
Though I'll respond with manners nice.
For all the while, if you but knew,
I really feel like fifty-two!
--Charles R. Humphrey Shreveport, LA.

COMMON SENSE

"Look to your future", a young man advised a 92 year old lady who was being urged to put her money in a long term investment.

"Sonny," she replied, at my house I don't even buy green bananas."

TODAY IS MY DAY

During a television interview, an 87 year-old woman was asked: "What were things like in your day?"

Smiling, the lady said firmly: "This is my day."

THE SENILITY PRAYER

Grant me the senility to forget the people I never liked anyway, the good fortune to run into the ones I do, and the eyesight to tell the difference.

VALUABLE THOUGHTS

A "has-been" is a person whose back faces the future.

Some people read just enough to stay misinformed.

There are few things as expensive as a cheap plumber.

Old postmasters never die, they just lose their zip.

Silence is one of the great arts of conversation.

Just because money cannot buy happiness doesn't mean you can't shop for a few chuckles.

Well BRED folks seem CRUSTY.

After all is said and done, often more is said

than done.

You can say one thing for ignorance—it sure causes a lot of interesting arguments.

Economics—If your outgo exceeds your income, your upkeep becomes your downfall.

FOR BETTER FOR WORSE; IN SICKNESS AND IN HEALTH. . . UNTIL

It was a busy morning, about 8:30AM, when an elderly gentleman in his 80's, arrived to have stitches removed from his thumb. He said he was in a hurry as he had an appointment at 9:00AM. I took his vital signs and had him take a seat, knowing it would be over an hour before someone would be able to see him. I saw him looking at his watch and decided, since I was not busy with another patient, I would evaluate his wound. On exam, it was well healed, so I talked to one of the doctors, got the needed supplies to remove his sutures and redress his wound.

While taking care of his wound, I asked him if he had another doctor's appointment this morning, as he was in such a hurry. The gentleman told me no, that he needed to go to the nursing home to eat breakfast with his wife. I inquired as to her health. He told me that she had been there for a while and that she was a victim of Alzheimer's Disease. As we talked, I asked if she would be upset if he was a bit late. He replied that she no longer knew who he was, that she had not recognized him in five years now. I was surprised , and asked him, "And you still go every morning, even though she doesn't know who you are?"

He smiled as he patted my hand and said, "She doesn't know me, but I still know who she is." I had to hold back tears as he left, I had goose bumps on my arm, and thought, "That is the kind of love I want in my life." True love is neither physical, nor romantic.

True love is an acceptance of all that is, has been, will be, and will not be. The happiest people don't necessarily have the best of everything; they just make the best of everything they have.

--Author Unknown

I'VE SURE GOTTEN OLD!

I've had two bypass surgeries, a hip replacement, new knees, fought prostate cancer and diabetes.

I'm half blind, can't hear anything quieter than a jet engine, take 40 different medications that make me dizzy, winded, and subject to blackouts.

Have bouts with dementia.

Have poor circulation; hardly feel my hands

and feet anymore.

Can't remember if I'm 85 or 92.
Have lost all my friends. But, thank God,
I still have my driver's license.

Jumping to conclusions is not half as good as an exercise as digging for the facts.

We should live and learn—trouble is that by the time we've learned, it's too late to live.

OLD FOLKS' TEXTING CODES

ATD -at the doctor.
BFF -best friend fell.
BTW -bring the wheelchair.
BYOT -bring your own teeth.
FWIW -forgot where I was.
GGPBL -gotta go, pacemaker battery low.
GHA -got heartburn again.
IMHO - IS MY HEARING AID ON?
LMDO -laughing my dentures out.
OMMR -on my massage recliner.
ROFLACGU -rolling on floor laughing and can't get up.

An elderly woman at an ATM asked me to

check her balance. So I pushed her over. Yep, she needs a walker.

The graveside service just barely finished, when there was a massive clap of thunder, followed by a tremendous bolt of lightning, accompanied by even more thunder rumbling in the distance.

The little old man looked at the preacher and calmly said, "Well......she's there."

A PRAYER FOR THOSE WHO LIVE ALONE

I live alone, dear Lord,
Stay by my side.
In all my daily needs
Be Thou my guide.
Grant me good health,
For that, indeed, I pray.
To carry on my work
From day to day.
Keep pure my mind,
My thoughts, my every deed.
Let me be kind, unselfish
In my neighbor's need.
Spare me from fire, from flood,
From thieves, from fear,
Malicious tongues,
And evil ones.
If sickness or an accident befall,
Then humbly, Lord, I pray,

Hear Thou my call,
And when I'm feeling low,
Or in despair,
Lift up my heart
And help me is my prayer.
I live alone, dear Lord,
Yet have no fear,
Because I feel Your Presence
Ever near.
--Anonymous

FOLKS DON'T KISS OLD PEOPLE ANY MORE

I still need the loving arms you put around me long ago when you were just a little child of four.

I still need your happy laughter and your kiss upon my brow, but folks don't kiss old people anymore.

My hair has turned to silver and my face lined with age where the traces of the years have gone before.

I still need the reassurance you long for as a child, but folks don't kiss old people any more.

When will you understand that I'm not really old at all, the thoughts that fill my mind are young as spring.

I can't erase my need for love, or take away the pain of loneliness that each new day may bring.

It would take a little time from busy chores you do; how I'd love to see you standing at my door.

I need to feel your gentle kiss upon my wrinkled face, but folks don't kiss old people any more.

SO TRUE

I owe a lot to my country,
On that I am very clear;
Especially when April comes
And tax filing time is here.

DAILY ROUTINE EXERCISE FOR SENIORS

Instructions for Exercise Block.

1. Place a block of wood on the floor in the center of the room.
2. Walk around the block twice, then sit down and relax.
3. If anyone asks have you exercised today, you can honestly say "I walked around the block twice."

POTS AND PANS

I frowned when our kids were tiny tots
And dragged out all the pans and pots.

But when our grandson follows suit,
I only smile and think it's cute!
--Margaret Wiedyke

ON LOSING A TOOTH

One day I found my five year old grandson Daniel crouched in a corner, sobbing hysterically.

"Honey, what in the world is wrong?" I asked.

When he could quiet down enough to speak, he pointed to a newly loose front tooth.

"Look!" he bawled. "I'm only five years old and already falling apart!"

--Bonnie Compton Hanson

STUFF

Every fall I start sorting my STUFF. There is a closest STUFF, drawer STUFF, attic STUFF, and basement STUFF. I separate the good STUFF from the bad STUFF. Then I STUFF the bad STUFF anywhere the STUFF is not too crowded until I decide if I will need the bad STUFF.

When the Lord calls me home, my children will want the good STUFF, but the bad STUFF -- STUFFED wherever there is room among all the other STUFF --will be STUFFED in bags and taken to the dump where all the other people's STUFF has been taken.

Whenever we have company, they always bring bags and bags of STUFF. When I visit my children, they always move their STUFF so I will have room for my STUFF. Their STUFF and my STUFF -- well, it would be so much easier to use their STUFF and leave my STUFF at home with the rest of my STUFF.

This Fall I had an extra closet built so I would have a place for all STUFF too good to throw away and too bad to keep with my good STUFF.

You may not have this problem, but I seem to spend a lot of time with STUFF. Food STUFF, cleaning STUFF, medicine STUFF, clothes STUFF, and outside STUFF.

Whatever would life be like if we didn't have all this STUFF?

Now there is all that STUFF we use to make us smell better than we do. There is the STUFF to make our hair look good; STUFF to make us look younger; STUFF to make us look healthier; STUFF to hold us in; and STUFF to fill us out.

There is STUFF to read, STUFF to play with, STUFF to entertain us, and STUFF to eat. We STUFF ourselves with the food STUFF.

Well, our lives are filled with STUFF -- good STUFF – bad STUFF -little STUFF -big STUFF -- useful STUFF – junky STUFF -- and everyone's STUFF. Now, when we leave all our STUFF and go to Heaven, whatever happens to our STUFF won't really matter. We will still have all the good STUFF God has prepared for us in Heaven.

P.S. *The author of this treatise is unknown -- or maybe he/she is stuck in his/her own STUFF.*

A perfect wife is one who doesn't expect a perfect husband.

A pessimist is one who feels bad when he feels good for fear he'll feel worse when he feels better.

POCKETBOOK INFORMATION

A grand-daughter tried to find out grandmother's age. Her grandmother gave no response. The little girl found her grandmother's purse and rummaged thru it. She ran to her grandmother and declared, "Now, I know how old you are. You are 76." Her Grandmother scolded her but the little girl continued, "Grandmother how come you got a F in sex?"

--Betty Gray, used by Permission

When you needed the discount, you paid full price. Now you get discounts on everything... movies, hotels, flights, but you're too tired to use them.

You forget names...but it's OK because other people forgot *they even knew you!!!*

The 5 pounds you wanted to lose is now 15 and you have a better chance of losing your keys than the 15 pounds.

BEATITUDES FOR FRIENDS OF THE AGED

Blessed are they who understand my faltering step and palsied hand.

Blessed are they who know that my ears today must strain to catch the things they say.

Blessed are they who seem to know that my ears are dim and wits are slow.

Blessed are they who looked away when coffee spilled at the table today.

Blessed are they with a cheery smile who stop to chat for a little while.

Blessed are they who never say "you've told that story twice today."

Blessed are they who know the ways to bring back memories of yesterdays.

Blessed are they who make it known that I'm loved, respected and not alone.

Blessed are they who know I'm at a loss to find the strength to carry the Cross.

Blessed are they who ease the days on my journey home.

Your spouse is counting on you to remember things you don't remember.

AT HOME AT THE HOLIDAY INN

No nursing home for us. We are checking into the Holiday Inn!

With the average cost for a nursing home care costing $188.00 per day, there is a better way when we get old & feeble. We have already checked on reservations at the Holiday Inn.

For a combined long term stay discount and senior discount, it's $49.23 per night. That leaves $138.77 a day for: Breakfast, lunch and dinner in any restaurant we want, or room service, laundry, gratuities and special TV movies. Plus, they provide a swimming pool, a workout room, a lounge and washer-dryer, etc.

Most have free toothpaste and razors, and all have free shampoo and soap. $5 worth of tips a day will have the entire staff scrambling to help you. They treat you like a customer, not a patient.

There is a city bus stop out front, and seniors ride free. The handicap bus will also pick you up (if you fake a decent limp). To meet other nice people, call a church bus on Sundays.

For a change of scenery, take the airport shuttle bus and eat at one of the nice restaurants there. While you're at the airport, fly somewhere. Otherwise, the cash keeps building up.

It takes months to get into decent nursing homes. Holiday Inn will take your reservation today. And you are not stuck in one place forever, you can move from Inn to Inn, or even from city to city. Want to see Hawaii ? They have a Holiday Inn there too.

TV broken? Light bulbs need changing? Need a mattress replaced? No problem . They fix everything, and apologize for the inconvenience.

The inn has a night security person and daily room service. The maid checks to see if you are ok. If not, they will call the undertaker or an ambulance. If you fall and break a hip, Medicare will pay for the hip and Holiday Inn will upgrade you to a suite for the rest of your life.

And no worries about visits from family. They will always be glad to find you, and probably check in for a few days mini-vacation. The grand kids can use the pool. What more can you ask for?

So, when we reach that golden age, we'll face it with a grin, AS WE WILL BE STAYING AT A HOLIDAY INN ! ! ! !

They also have wireless capability, so I'll be reachable at my regular Gmail address.

SITTING BY THE FIRE

An old man sat by the open fire,
And dreamed the years away;
While outside in the battle of life
Many perished in the toils of day.
He never did any good, nor did he
Ever do any wrong-
He just sat by the open fire,
And dreamed, the whole day long.
Now he's left a vacant chair,
And they say he's gone up higher,
But if he still does what he used to do,
He's still sitting by the fire.

INVOLVEMENT

Dear Everybody,

This is a story about four people named Anybody, Everybody, Somebody and Nobody.

There was an important job to be done and Everybody was asked to do it. Anybody could do it, but Nobody did it. Somebody was angry about that because it was Everybody's job.

Everybody thought that Anybody could do it and Nobody realized that Everybody wouldn't do it. It ended up that Everybody blamed Somebody when actually Nobody blamed Everybody.

Does this sound familiar to Anybody?

--(signed) "Somebody"

A PUN POEM (UNTITLED)

Where can a man buy a cap for his knee?
Or a key to the lock of his hair?
Should your eyes be called an academy
Because there are pupils there?
In the crown of your head, what jewels are found? .
Who travels the bridge of your nose?
Could you use in shingling the roof of your mouth
The nails on the end of your toes?
Could the crook in your elbow be sent to jail?
If so, what did be do?
How can you sharpen your shoulder blades,
I'll be darned if I know, do you?
Can you sit in the shade of the palm of your hand

And play on the drum of your ear?
Do the calves of our legs eat the corn on our
toes,
Then why does it grow on the ear?

WHAT TYPE OF A "BONE" ARE YOU?

Someone has said that there are four kind of "BONES" in every organization.

There are the "WISHBONES" who spend their time wishing someone else would do the work.

There are the "JAWBONES" who do all the talking, but very little else.

Next, there are the "KNUCKLEBONES" who knock everything anyone ever tries to do.

And finally, there are the "BACKBONES" who get under the load and do all the work.

WHICH KIND ARE YOU?

A SECOND CHILDHOOD

Two elderly gentlemen from a retirement center were sitting on a bench under a tree when one turns to the other and says: "Slim, I'm 83 years old now and I'm just full of aches and pains. I know you're about my age. How do you feel?"

Slim says, "I feel just like a newborn baby."

"Really! Like a newborn baby!"

"Yep. No hair, no teeth, and I think I just wet

my pants."

FOLGERS COFFEE AD EFFECTIVE

A grandmother was surprised by her 7-year-old grandson one morning. He had made her coffee. She tasted what was the worst cup of coffee in her life, but because it had been made with love, she did not let on.

When she finally finished it, she noticed that there were three little green Army men toys in her cup.

She said to her grandson, "Honey, what are the Army men doing in my coffee?"

He replied, "Grandma, it says on TV -- 'The best part of waking up is soldiers in your cup.'"

A woman checked in at the pearly gates and asked to join her former husband, Walter Smith. Saint Peter said, "We have five million Walter Smiths. Give us a little clue."

The woman said, "My Walter is bald and has blue eyes, and he said that if I ever married again he'd turn over in his grave."

Saint Peter motioned an angel forward. "Take her to Whirling Walter!

A diabetic diet is easy to handle.
Skip the cake, and eat the candle

About the time your income is fixed, your body begins to need repairs.

COME JOURNEY WITH ME DOWN "MEMORY LANE"

To those great days of "yesteryear"
When life held such simple pleasures
And less of our modern day fear!
The "streetcar" rides to Camden Park,
Movie "serials" each Saturday noon
When we watched the antics of 'ole Tom Mix,
Hoot Gibson, and Daniel Boone!
I remember the fun of "belling"
Each neighborhood "newlywed",
Oh! What joy it was back then
To rouse them from their bed!
I remember when "gay" meant "happy"
And "grass" was something you "mowed"
When "pot" was a vessel to hold your "stew",
And a "weed" was a thing you "pulled".
Oh! to turn back the time to "days of yore",
And "memories" I sweetly recall
Would be a "journey" I'd treasure,
As I recaptured the thrill of it all!
– Art Poll

JOINING A FITNESS CLUB

I feel like my body has gotten totally out of shape, so I got my doctor's permission to join a fitness club and start exercising.

I decided to take an aerobics class for seniors.

I bent, twisted, gyrated, jumped up and down, and perspired for an hour. But, by the time I got my got my leotards on, the class was over.

My mind is like lightening: one brilliant flash and it is gone.

TODAY'S GRANDMA

(Modern Version)

The old rocking chair will be empty today
For Grandma is no longer in it.
She is off in her car to her office or shop
And buzzes around every minute.
No one can shove Grandma back up on the shelf
She is versatile, forceful, dynamic,
That isn't a pie in the oven, you know--
Her baking today is ceramic.
You won't see her trundling off early to bed.

From a place in a warm chimney nook
Her typewriter clackety-clacks through the night
For Grandma is writing a book.

She isn't content with crumbs of old thought
With meager and second-hand knowledge.
So don't bring your mending for Grandma to do
For Grandma has gone back to college!
--Author Unknown

My next house will have no kitchen—just vending machines and a large trash can.

As you slide down the banister of life, may
The splinters never point the wrong way.

The only time the world beats a path to your door is if you are in the bathroom.

The sole purpose of a child's middle name is so he can tell when he is in trouble.

If you think there is good in everybody, you haven't met everybody.

IT STAGGERS THE MIND, EH

This 80 year old woman was arrested for shop lifting.

When she went before the judge in Cincinnati he asked her,

"What did you steal"

She replied, "A can of peaches."

The judge then asked her why she had stolen the can of peaches and she replied that she was hungry.

The judge then asked her how many peaches were in the can.

She replied, "6."

The judge said, "Then I will give you 6 days in jail."

Before the judge could conclude the trial, the woman's husband spoke up and asked the judge if he could say something.

The judge said, "What is it"

The husband said, "She also stole a can of peas."

MR. POSTMASTER GENERAL

Why do they put pictures of criminals up in the Post Office? What are we supposed to do, write to these men? Why don't they just put their pictures on the postage stamps so the mailmen could look for them while they deliver the mail? Or better yet, arrest them while they are taking their pictures!

Employment application blanks always ask 'who is to be notified in case of an emergency.' I think you should write, "A Good Doctor!"

I was thinking about old age and decided that old age is 'when you still have something on the ball, but you are just too tired to bounce it.'

TAKE TIME RECIPE

Take Time to think ...
It is the source of power.
Take Time to play ...
It is the secret of perpetual youth
Take Time to read ...
It is the fountain of wisdom.
Take Time to pray ...
It is the greatest power on earth.
Take Time to love and be loved...
It is a God-given privilege.
Take Time to be friendly ...
It is the road to happiness.
Take Time to laugh ...

It is the music of the soul.
Take Time to give ...
It is too short a day to be selfish.
Take Time to work ...
It is the price of success.
Take Time to do charity ...
It is the key to heaven.

A FREE RIDE

Hospital regulations require a wheel chair for patients being discharged. However, while working as a student nurse, I found one elderly gentleman already dressed and sitting on the bed with a suitcase at his feet, who insisted he didn't need my help to leave the hospital.

After a chat about rules being rules, he reluctantly let me wheel him to the elevator.

On the way down I asked him if his wife was meeting him.

"I don't know," he said. "She's still upstairs in the bathroom changing out of her hospital gown."

SHE KNEW THE ANSWER

An elderly couple had dinner at another couple's house, and after eating, the wives left the table and went into the kitchen.

The two gentlemen were talking, and one said, "Last night we went out to a new restaurant and it was really great. I would recommend it very highly."

The other man said, "What is the name of the restaurant?"

The first man thought and thought and finally said, "What is the name of that flower you give to someone you love? You know... the one that's red and has thorns?"

"Do you mean a rose?"

"Yes, that's the one," replied the man. He then turned towards the kitchen and yelled, "Rose, what's the name of that restaurant we went to last night?"

Your husband sleeps better on a lounge chair with the TV blaring than he does in bed. It's called his "pre-sleep".

Remember when your mother said, "Wear clean underwear in case you GET in an accident?" Now you bring clean underwear in case you HAVE an accident!

Now that your husband has retired...you'd give anything if he'd find a job!

You have 3 sizes of clothes in your closet...2 of which you will never wear.

OLD MEN ARE RESOURCEFUL

An elderly gentleman had serious hearing problems for a number of years. He went to the doctor and the doctor was able to have him fitted for a set of hearing aids that allowed the gentleman to hear 100%.

The elderly gentleman went back in a month to the doctor and the doctor said, "Your hearing is perfect. Your family must be really pleased that you can hear again."

The gentleman replied, "Oh, I haven't told my family yet.

I just sit around and listen to the conversations. I've changed my will three times!"

An elderly woman decided to prepare her will and told her preacher she had two final requests. First, she wanted to be cremated, and second, she wanted her ashes scattered over WalMart.

"WalMart," the preacher exclaimed. "Why WalMart?"

"Then I'll be sure my daughters visit me twice a week."

By the time the world is your oyster, you may lose the strength to open the shell.

You know you're getting old when that "come hither" look turns into "get out of here" look.

YOUR CONVERSATION

You speak of nothing but your ills...
Your different doctors...different pills;
And whimper for a solid hour
About your stomach, which is sour!
You shun all subjects that are cheerier
And frankly discuss your whole interior!

SELFISH MAN

A lady in Knoxville, TN was granted a divorce after she showed the court a postcard addressed to her on which her husband had written a little verse.

"Your eyes may shine,
Your teeth may grit,
But none of my money
Will you get.
Phooey on you."

Anyone who thinks he knows all the answers just isn't up-to-date on the questions.

LIFE

Life is a mixture of sunshine and rain,
Teardrops and laughter

Pleasures and pain,
We can't have all bright days
But one thing is true,
No cloud is so dark
That the sun can't shine thru.

FAITH HEALER OR PHONY

A patient tells the doctor, "I've been going to a faith healer, but I wasn't getting any better."

The doctor smiled and said, "And what dumb advice did this phony give you?"

"He told me to come see you," replied the new patient.

Did you ever notice the Roman Numerals for forty (40) are "XL"?

If you can smile when things go wrong, you have someone in mind to blame.

COMPLAINTS

My teeth don't fit,
My ears don't hear,
My eyes are half gone,
What am I doing here?

Taking up space,
A burden to my kids
What's there to do
When Life is on skids?

My muscles ache,
My head's full of bumps,
My stomach's out of order,
My leg's have the "jumps!"

Beyond all those things,
Guess I can't complain!
Thank you Lord, for the good things,
So far, I don't need a cane!

Give me a shopping cart in a store,
I can fly right down the aisles,
A little bit of money,
And I'll pass out lots of smiles.
--Claudia M. Peters 5/25/93

I'M AS I USED TO BE

It's passing strange that
Relentless years exact a toll
From everyone but ME;
The others change, but on the whole,
I'm as I used to be.

THEIR swelling bulk, THEIR thinning hair
THEIR wrinkles all surprise me;

In fact, they're altered so, I swear
THEY fail to recognize ME.!
--John McGiffert

Some people try to turn back their odometers. Not me, I want people to know "why" I look this way. I've traveled a long way and some of the roads weren't paved.

When you are dissatisfied and would
Like to go back to youth,
Think of Algebra.

The older we get, the fewer things seem worth waiting in line for.

SENIORS, THE NEW ALPHABET

A is for apple, and B is for boat,
That used to be right, but now it won't float!
Age before beauty is what we once said,
But let's be a bit more realistic instead.

Now:
A is for arthritis;
B is the bad back,
C is the chest pains, perhaps cardiac?

D is for dental decay and decline,
E is for eyesight--can't read that top line!
F is for fissures and water retention,
G is for gas, which I'd rather not mention.

H is high blood pressure--I'd prefer low;
I is for incisions with scars you can show.
J is for joints, out of socket, won't mend,
K is for knees that crack when they bend.

L is for lost hearing--now what did you say?
M is for memory lapses occurring all day.
N is neurolga, in nerves way down low;
O is for osteo, the bones that don't grow!

P for prescriptions, I have quite a few;
Just give me a pill and I'll be good as new!
Q is for queasy. Is it fatal or flu?
R is for reflux--one meal turns to two.

S is for sleepless nights, counting my fears,
T for tinnitus; there are bells in my ears!
U is for urinary; big troubles with flow;
V is for vertigo--that's "dizzy," you know.

W is for worry. Now what's going 'round?
X is for x-ray and what might be found.
Y is for another year I'm left behind,
Z is for zest that I still have--in my mind.

--From KYOWVA Evangelistic Association Newsletter

WRONG WAY DRIVER

As a senior citizen was driving down the freeway his car phone rang.

Answering, he heard his wife's voice urgently warning him: "Herman, I just heard on the news that there's a car going the wrong way on 280 Interstate. Please be careful!"

"It's not just one car," answered Herman. "It's hundreds of them."

Did you ever notice: When you put the 2 words "The" and "IRS" together it spells "Theirs"

CHRISTMAS AT ROCKWAY REST

'Twas the night before Christmas at
Rockaway Rest
And all of us seniors were looking our best.
Our glasses, how sparkly, our wrinkles,
how merry;
Our punch bowl had prune juice plus three
drops of Sherry.

A bed sock was taped to each walker, in
hope,
That Santa would bring us soft candy and
soap.
We surely were lucky to be there with
friends
Secure in this residence and in our
Depends.

Our grandkids had sent us some
Christmassy Crafts,
Like Angels in snowsuits and penguins on
rafts.
The Dental Assistant had borrowed our
teeth,
And from them, she'd crafted a holiday
wreath.

The bedpans, so shiny, all stood in a row,
Reflecting our Candle's magnificent
glow.
Our supper, so festive - the joy wouldn't
stop,
Was creamy warm oatmeal with sprinkles
on top.

Our salad was Jell-o, so jiggly and great,
Then puree of fruitcake was spooned on
each plate.
The social director then had us play games,

Like "Where are you living?" and, "What
is your name?"

Old Grandfather Looper was feeling his oats
proclaiming that reindeer were nothing
but goats.
Our resident wanderer was tied to her
chair,
In hopes that at bedtime she still would be
there.

Security lights on the new-fallen snow
Made outdoors seem noon to the old
folks below.
Then out on the porch there arose such a
clatter
But we are so deaf that it just didn't matter.

A strange little fellow flew in through the
door,
Then tripped on the sill and fell flat on the
floor.
'Twas just our director, all togged out in
red,
He jiggled and chuckled and patted each
head.

We knew from the way that he strutted and
jived
Our Social Security checks had arrived.

We sang - how we sang - in our monotone
croak,
Till the clock ticked out its soft eight p.m.
stroke.

And soon we were snuggling deep in our
beds
While nurses distributed nocturnal meds.
And so ends our Christmas at Rock-Away
Rest.
Before long you'll be with us, we wish you
the best!
--Author Unknown-

A NEW HEARING AID

A man was telling his neighbor, I just bought a new hearing aid. "It cost me four thousand dollars, but its state of the art."

"Really," answered the neighbor. "What kind is it?"

"Twelve thirty."

Card games can be expensive, but then so can any game where you hold hands.

A CLEAR MISUNDERSTANDING

Morris, an 83 year old man, went to the doctor to get a physical.

A few days later the doctor saw Morris walking down the street with a gorgeous young lady on his arm.

A couple of days later the doctor spoke to the man a said, "You're really doing great, aren't you?"

Morris replied, "Just doing what you said, Doctor, 'Get a hot mamma and be cheerful.'"

The doctor said "I didn't say that. I said, 'You've got a heart mummer. Be careful.'"

I FORGOT HER NAME

An elderly gent was invited to his old friends' home for dinner one evening. He was impressed by the way his buddy preceded every request to his wife with endearing terms-Honey, My Love, Darling, Sweetheart, Pumpkin, etc. The couple had been married almost 70 years and clearly, they were still very much in love.

While the wife was in the kitchen, the man leaned over and said to his host, "I think its wonderful that, after all these years, you still call your wife those loving pet names."

The old man hung his head. “I have to tell you the truth,” he said. “I forgot her name about 10 years ago.”

A group of Americans were traveling by tour bus through Holland. As they stopped at a cheese farm, a young guide led them through the process of cheese making, explaining that goat's milk was used.

She showed the group a lively hillside where many goats were grazing. “These,” she explained “are the older goats, put out to pasture when they no longer produce.”

She then asked, “What do you do in America with your old goats?”

A spry old gentleman answered, “They send us on bus tours!”

Adolescence is the time in a boy’s life when he notices that a girl notices that he is noticing her.

THE WAY IT WAS----1935

Just think! This was before polio shots, penicillin and antibiotics, nylon, dacron and polyester. No TV, VCR'S, Radar, fluorescent lights, credit cards or ball point pens. Time sharing meant togetherness, not condos. A chip was just a piece of wood, hardware meant hardware and software wasn't even a word. We didn't have hula hoops, frisbees, video games or home computers and word processors.

We had no drip-dry clothes, panty hose, or cup sizing bras, and cleavage was something the butcher did. No ice makers, electric ice cream freezers, electric blankets or deep freezers. Other than our MOTHER, a dishwasher was someone who worked in a restaurant, and a clothes dryer was a wire between two poles in the backyard. Men didn't wear long hair or ear rings and women didn't wear pants with the exception of the unmentionable kind and good women did not smoke in public.

In our day, closets were for clothes, not coming out of. Bunnies were small rabbits and rabbits were not Volkswagons. We were before pizza, Cheerios, frozen orange juice and packaged foods. Packaged biscuits and McDonald's were unheard of, except for Old McDonalds Farm. We thought fast food was what you ate during Lent. No polaroid cameras, FM radios or tape recorders, and best of all - no electronic MUSIC AMPLIFIERS (Thank you God). Remember when a nickel would buy a stamp and two post cards; and with a dime you could go shopping at the 5 and 10 cent store?

Not in our wildest imagination could we foresee making a trip in a jet plane from California to New York in four hours. Come to think about it, jet planes, space-craft and men walking on the moon were some things we read about in the comic strips. In our day, COKE was something you drank, grass was mowed, and POT was something you cooked in.

We hadn't heard of the forty-hour-work week, the minimum wage, or age and unemployment insurance. We made do with what we had and we had very little. We got married first, then lived together. Gee, how quaint we were! We were the last generation that was so dumb to think you had to have, or needed, a husband to have a baby. We sure lived in a different world, but to us, 1935 was the year. IT WAS PART OF THE GOOD OLD DAYS!

PINK CHIFFON DRESS

I saw a dress on sale one day while strolling
through the mall
It was the dreamiest one I'd ever seen, but
DARN it was too small.
I stood and gazed upon that dress, like I was in
a trance

I pictured myself wearing it to our club's fancy
dance.
I turned and went inside the shop and told the
clerk I'd take it.
I knew I couldn't wear it now, but I was sure
I'd make it.
For our club's dance was two months off-that
gave me lots of time
I'd cut calories and exercise, then I'd be in my
prime.
The dress was in a plastic bag and hanging in
plain sight
I made real sure I'd see it every morning, noon
and night!
The two months time is nearly gone, my, how
time flies by.
I'll have to get my courage up and give that
dress a try!
With fear and anticipation, I removed it from
the bag.
From head to foot I trembled, I felt as limp as a
rag,
I told myself, "Now hold on, girl, you really are
a mess.
Why get so excited over just one sheer pink
dress?"
But I had grown to love that dress and I had
longed to wear it.
If I fail now my heart will break, I don't think I
could bear it.

I've tried real hard, not cheated once, and never was a gainer.
Ok, it's on and half zipped up
O my gosh, now it's too big!!!

Advice for the day: If you have a lot of tension and you get a headache, do what it says on the aspirin bottle: "Take two aspirin" and "Keep away from children."

If you are going to try cross-country skiing, start with a small country.

AFTER ALL THESE YEARS, FOR THAT I AM THANKFUL

It doesn't seem to get any better, but it doesn't get any worse either.
For that, I am thankful.
There are no more pictures to be taken, but there are memories to be cherished.
For that, I am thankful.
There is a missing chair at the table, but the circle of family gathers close.
For that, I am thankful.
The turkey is smaller, but there is still stuffing.
For that, I am thankful.
The pain is still there, but it lasts only moments.

For that, I am thankful.
The calendar still turns, the holidays still appear and they still cost too much. And I am still here.
For that, I am thankful.
The room is still empty, the soul still aches, but the heart remembers.
For that, I am thankful.
The guests still come, the dishes pile up, but the dishwasher works.
For that, I am thankful.
The name is still missing, the words still unspoken, but the silence is shared.
For that, I am thankful.
The snow still falls, the sled still waits, and the spirit still wants to.
For that, I am thankful.
The stillness remains, but the sadness is smaller.
For that, I am thankful.
The moment is gone, but the love is forever.
For THAT I am blessed. For THAT, I am grateful.
Love was once (and still is) a part of my being.
For THAT I am living.
I am living.
For THAT I am Thankful.
--Darcie Sims, Ph. D.

Don't cry because it's over, smile because it happened.

Pain and Suffering are inevitable but Misery is optional.

Yesterday is history,
Tomorrow is a mystery,
Today is a gift,
That's why it is called, THE PRESENT

A good exercise for the heart is to bend down and help another up.

THE SPARROW AT STARBUCKS

It was chilly in Manhattan but warm inside the Starbucks shop on 51st Street and Broadway, just a skip up from Times Square. Early November weather in New York City holds only the slightest hint of the bitter chill of late December and January, but it's enough to send the masses crowding indoors to vie for available space and warmth.

For a musician, it's the most lucrative Starbucks location in the world, I'm told, and consequently, the tips can be substantial if you play your tunes right. Apparently, we were striking all the right chords that night, because our basket was almost overflowing.

It was a fun, low-pressure gig and I was

playing keyboard and singing backup for my friend who also added rhythm with an arsenal of percussion instruments. We mostly did pop songs from the '40s to the '90s with a few original tunes thrown in. During our emotional rendition of the classic, "If You Don't Know Me by Now," I noticed a lady sitting in one of the lounge chairs across from me. She was swaying to the beat and singing along.

After the tune was over, she approached me. "I apologize for singing along on that song. Did it bother you?" she asked. "No," I replied. "We love it when the audience joins in. Would you like to sing up front on the next selection?" To my delight, she accepted my invitation. "You choose," I said. "What are you in the mood to sing?"

"Well. Do you know any hymns?"

Hymns? This woman didn't know who she was dealing with. I cut my teeth on hymns. Before I was even born, I was going to church. I gave our guest singer a knowing look. "Name one."

"Oh, I don't know. There are so many good ones. You pick one.

"Okay," I replied. "How about, 'His Eye is on the Sparrow'?"

My new friend was silent, her eyes averted. Then she fixed her eyes on mine again and said, "Yeah. Let's do that one."

She slowly nodded her head, put down her

purse, straightened her jacket and faced the center of the shop. With my two-bar setup, she began to sing:

"Why should I be discouraged?
Why should the shadows come?"

The audience of coffee drinkers was transfixed. Even the gurgling noises of the cappuccino machine ceased as the employees stopped what they were doing to listen. The song rose to its conclusion:

"I sing because I'm happy;
I sing because I'm free.
For His eye is on the sparrow
And I know He watches me."

Holy moment when the last note was sung, the applause became a crescendo and a deafening roar that would have rivaled a sold-out crowd at Carnegie Hall.

Embarrassed, the woman tried to shout over the din, "Oh, y'all go back to your coffee. I didn't come in here to do a concert. I just came in here to get somethin' to drink, just like you!"

But the ovation continued. I embraced my new friend. "You, my dear, have made my whole year. That was beautiful."

"Well, it's funny that you picked that particular hymn," she said.

"Why is that?"

"Well," she hesitated again, "that was my daughter's favorite song."

"Really!" I exclaimed.

"Yes," she said, and then grabbed my hands. By this time, the applause had subsided and it was business as usual. "She was 16. She died of a brain tumor last week."

I said the first thing that found its way through my stunned silence.

"Are you going to be okay?"

She smiled through tear-filled eyes and squeezed my hands. "I'm gonna be okay. I've just got to keep trusting the Lord and singing his songs, and everything's gonna be just fine."

She picked up her bag, gave me her card, and then she was gone.

Was it just a coincidence that we happened to be singing in that particular coffee shop on that particular November night?

Coincidence that this wonderful lady just happened to walk into that particular shop? Coincidence that of all the hymns to choose from, I just happened to pick the very hymn that was the favorite of her daughter, who had died just the week before?

I refuse to believe it. God has been arranging encounters in human history since the beginning of time, and it's no stretch for me to imagine that he could reach into a coffee shop in midtown Manhattan and turn an ordinary gig into a revival.

It was a great reminder that if we keep trusting him and singing his songs, everything's going to be fine.

--John Thomas Oaks
Used by Permission

The bubbling brook would lose its song if you removed the rocks.

Happiness comes through doors you didn't even know you left open.

ELVIS SERENADE

These are the words Elvis would be singing if he was with us today.

"Are you lonesome tonight, does your
tummy feel tight?
Did you bring your Mylanta and Tums?
Does your memory stray, to that bright
sunny day,
When you had all you teeth with your
gums?

Is your hairline receding? Are your eyes
growing dim?
Hysterectomy for her and it's prostate for
him.

Does your back give you pain...Do your knees predict rain?
Tell me dear, are you lonesome tonight?

Is your blood pressure up, your cholesterol down?
Are you eating low fat cuisine?
All that oat bran and fruit, Metamucil to boot,
Keeps you like a well oiled machine.

If it's football or baseball...he sure knows the score.
Yes, he knows where it's at ...but forgets what it's for.
So your gallbladder's gone. But his gout lingers on.
Tell me dear are you lonesome tonight?

When you're hungry, he's not, when you're cold, then he's hot.
Then you start that old thermostat war.
When you turn out the light, he goes left, you go right.
Then you get his great symphonic snore.

He was once so romantic, and witty and tan.
How'd he turn out to be such a cranky old man?
So don't take any bets, this is as good as it

gets.
Tell me dear are you lonesome tonight?"
(Author unknown)

HYMNS FOR THOSE OVER 70

"Precious Lord, Take My Hand." And Help Me Up.

"Count Your Many Birthdays." Count Them One By One.

"Go Tell It On A Mountain." But Speak Up.

"Give Me The Old 'Timers' Religion."

"Blessed 'Insurance."

"Guide Me O Thou Great Lord God." I've Forgotten Where I've Parked The Truck.

SENIORS ARE NOT GUILTY

Senior citizens are constantly being criticized for every conceivable deficiency of the modern world, real or imaginary. We know we take responsibility for all we have done and do not blame others.

HOWEVER, upon reflection, we would like to point out that it was NOT the senior citizens who took:

The melody out of music,
The pride out of appearance,
The courtesy out of driving,
The romance out of love,
The commitment out of marriage,

The responsibility out of parenthood,
The togetherness out of the family,
The learning out of education,
The service out of patriotism,
The Golden Rule from rulers,
The nativity scene out of cities,
The civility out of behavior,
The refinement out of language,
The dedication out of employment,
The prudence out of spending,
The ambition out of achievement, or
God out of government and school.

And we certainly are NOT the ones who eliminated patience and tolerance from personal relationships and interactions with others!! And, we do understand the meaning of patriotism, and remember those who have fought and died for our country. Does anyone under the age of 50 know the lyrics to the *Star Spangled Banner* or *O Canada*? Just look at the Seniors with tears in their eyes and pride in their hearts as they stand at attention on Veteran's Day and our great country's birthday.

I WONDER ABOUT THINGS

If lawyers are disbarred and clergymen defrocked, doesn't it follow that electricians can be delighted, musicians denoted, cowboys deranged, models deposed and dry cleaners depressed? Laundry workers could decrease, eventually becoming depressed and depleted!

Even more, bed makers will be debunked, baseball players will be debased, landscapers will be deflowered, bulldozer operators will be degraded, organ donors will be delivered, software engineers will be detested, the BVD company will be debriefed, and even musical composers will eventually decompose.

On a more positive note though, perhaps we can hope politicians will be devoted.

YES, I'M A SENIOR CITIZEN

I'm the life of the party...even when it lasts until 8 p.m.

I'm very good at opening child-proof caps with a hammer.

I'm usually interested in going home before I get where I'm going.

I'm good on trips for at least an hour without my aspirin, beano and antacid.

I'm the first one to find the bathroom wherever I go.

I'm smiling all the time because I can't hear a word you are saying.

I'm very good at telling stories...over and over and over.

I'm aware that other people's grandchildren are not as bright as mine.

I'm so cared for: long-term care, eye care,
private care, dental care....
I'm awake many hours before my body
allows me to get up.
I'm not grouchy, I just don't like traffic,
waiting, crowds, lawyers, loud music,
unruly kids, Jenny Craig, Toyota
commercials, barking dogs, politicians
and a few other things I can't seem to
remember right now.
I'm wrinkled, saggy and lumpy, and that's
just my left leg.
I'm positive I did housework correctly, before
my mate retired.
I'm sure everything I can't find is in a safe
secure place, somewhere.
I'm having trouble remembering simple
words like.......
I'm sure they are making adults much
younger these days, and when did they let
kids become policemen?
And, how can my kids be older than I feel
sometimes?
I' m realizing that aging is not for sissies.
I'm anti-everything now; anti-fat, anti-smoke,
anti-noise, anti-inflammation....
I'm walking more (to the bathroom) and
enjoying it less.
I'm sure they are making adults much
younger these days.

I'm in the initial state of my golden years: SS, CD's, IRA's, AARP.....
I'm wondering...if you're old as you feel, how could I be alive at 135?
I'm supporting all movements now...by eating bran, prunes and raisins.
I'm a walking storeroom of facts . . . I've just lost the storeroom.
Yes, I'm a SENIOR CITIZEN and I think I am having the time of my life!

Why is it that every time I lose weight, it finds me again?

OVERHEARD IN A BEAUTY PARLOR

A lady commented that if she died, her husband would be married in a week. The operator said "How do you know that?" And the answer was, "Well my husband likes eggs every morning for breakfast and he does not know how to cook. He'll be out looking right away."

From across the room came a voice, "Scrambled or fried?"

I signed up for an exercise class and was told to wear loose-fitting clothing. If I HAD any loose-fitting clothing, I wouldn't have signed up in the first place!

When I was young we used to go "skinny dipping," now I just "chunky dunk."

Stress is when you wake up screaming and then you realize you haven't fallen asleep yet.

My husband says I never listen to him. At least I think that's what he said.

If raising children was going to be easy, it never would have started with something called labor!

RELIEVE A LITTLE STRESS

An elderly man in North Carolina had owned a large farm for several years. He had a large pond in the back, fixed up really nice, along with some picnic tables, horseshoe courts, and some apple and peach trees. The pond was properly shaped and fixed up for swimming when it was built.

One evening the old farmer decided to go down to the pond, as he hadn't been there for a while, and look it over. He grabbed a five gallon bucket to bring back some fruit.

As he neared the pond, he heard voices shouting and laughing with glee. When he came closer, he realized it was a bunch of young women skinny-dipping in his pond. He made the women aware of his presence and they all went to the deep end to shield themselves.

One of the women shouted to him, "We're not coming out until you leave!"

The old man frowned and replied, "I didn't come down here to watch you ladies swim naked or make you get out of the pond naked." Holding the bucket up he said, "I'm here to feed the alligator."

Moral of the story: Old men may move slow but can still think fast.

HOW MANY DO YOU REMEMBER?

Head lights dimmer switches on the floor.
Ignition switches on the dashboard.
Heaters mounted on the inside of the fire wall.
Real ice boxes.
Pant leg clips for bicycles without chain guards.
Soldering irons you heat on a gas burner.
Using hand signals for cars without turn signals.
Blackjack chewing gum.
Wax Coke-shaped bottles with colored sugar water.
Candy cigarettes.

Soda pop machines that dispensed glass bottles.
Coffee shops or diners with tableside juke boxes.
Home milk delivery in glass bottles with cardboard stoppers.
Party lines.
Newsreels before the movie.
P.F. Flyers.
Butch wax.
Telephone numbers with a word prefix (Olive-6933).

GETTING OLD?

You tell me I am getting old;
I tell you that's not so!
The "house" I live in is worn out-
And that, of course, I know.
It's been in use a long, long while;
It's weathered many a gale;
I'm really not surprised you think
It's getting somewhat frail.

The color's changing on the roof,
The windows getting dim,
The walls, a bit transparent
And is looking rather thin.
The foundation's not so steady,
Weaker than it used to be;
My "house" is getting shaky,

But my “house” isn't me!

A few short years can't make me old-
I feel I'm in my youth;
Eternity lies just ahead,
And life, and joy, and, truth.
I'm going to live forever then;
Life will go on-it's grand!
You tell me that I'm getting old?
You just don't understand

The dweller in my little “house”
Is young and bright and free-
Just starting on a life to last
Throughout eternity.
You only view the outside shell,
That's all that most folk see.
You tell me I am getting old?
You've mixed my house with me!
--Donna Johnson in *Harvester*

GOSH. I'M RICH!

Silver in the Hair
Gold in the Teeth
Stones in the Kidneys
Sugar in the Blood
Lead in my Behind
Iron in the Arteries
And an inexhaustible supply of Natural Gas.

I never thought I'd accumulate such wealth!!.

Always Remember This:
You don't stop laughing because you grow old,
You grow old because you stop laughing.

NOW THAT I AM OLDER, HERE'S WHAT I'VE DISCOVERED

1. I started out with nothing, and I still have most of it.
2. My wild oats have turned into prunes and All Bran.
3. I finally got my head together; now my body is falling apart.
4. Funny, I don't remember being absent minded...
5. All reports are in; Life is now officially unfair.
6. If all is not lost, where is it?
7. It is easier to get older than it is to get wiser.
8. I wish the buck stopped here; I sure could use a few.
9. If God wanted me to touch my toes, he would have put them on my knees.

10. When I'm finally holding all the cards, why does everyone decide to play chess?
11. Some mistakes are too much fun to make only once.
12. The only time the world beats a path to your door is when you're in the bathroom.
13. It's hard to make a comeback when you haven't been anywhere.
14. It has not been hard meeting expenses; they are everywhere I look.
15. I spend more time thinking about the HEREAFTER. I go some where to get something and then wonder what I am hereafter.
16. Whatever hits the fan will not be distributed evenly.
17. Sometimes you're the dog and sometimes you're the hydrant.
18. If it wasn't for stress, I'd have no energy at all.
19. There are always some things to be thankful for--for example: Aren't we glad that wrinkles do not hurt?
20. If ignorance is bliss, why aren't more people happy?
21. The older you get, the tougher it is to lose weight, because by then your body and your fat have become really good friends.
22. I think about exercise but if I lie down, it goes away.

23. I have to exercise early in the morning before my brain finds out what I am doing.
24. The advantage of exercising every day is that you die healthier.
25. It is well documented that for every minute of exercise, you add a minute to your life. This enables you, at 85 years of age to spend an additional five months in a nursing home at $5,000 per month.
26. My friend tells me how good walking is for your health. His Grandmother started walking five miles a day at the age of 65. I found out that she is now 97 years old but they have no idea where she ended up.
27. I know that God won't give me more than I can handle, but sometimes I just wish He didn't trust me so much.
28. Live each day as if it were your last...One of these days you'll be right.
29. Don't cry because it is over, smile because it happened.
30. A man is not poor if he can laugh.

Several years ago to commemorate her birthday, actress/vocalist, Julie Andrews made a special appearance at Manhattan 's Radio City Music Hall for the benefit of the AARP.

One of the musical numbers she performed was "My Favorite Things" from the legendary movie “Sound Of Music”. Here are the lyrics she used:

Maalox and nose drops and needles for knitting.
Walkers and handrails and new dental fittings,
Bundles of magazines tied up in string,
These are a few of my favorite things.

Cadillacs and cataracts and hearing aids and glasses,
Polident and Fixodent and false teeth in glasses,
Pacemakers, golf balls and porches with swings,
These are a few of my favorite things.
When the pipes leak,
When the bones creak.
When the knees go bad,
I simply remember my favorite things
And then I don't feel so bad.

Hot tea and crumpets and corn pads for bunions,
No spicy hot food cooked with onions,
Bathrobes and heat pads and hot meals they bring,
These are a few of my favorite things.

Back pains, confused brains, and no fear of sinnin',
Thin bones and fractures and hair that is thinnin',
And we won't mention our short shrunken frames,
When we remember our favorite things.

When the joints ache, when the hips break,
When the eyes grow dim,
Then I remember the great life I've had,
And then I don't feel so bad.

Aging is like a hot bath, the longer you stay in it, the more wrinkled you get.

AN ANNIVERSARY EXPERIENCE

No one believes seniors . . . everyone thinks they are senile.

An Elderly couple was celebrating their sixtieth anniversary. The couple had married as childhood sweethearts and had moved back to their old neighborhood after they retired. Holding hands they walked back to their old school. It was not locked, so they entered, and found the old desk they'd shared, where Andy had carved "I love you, Sally."

On their way back home, a bag of money fell out of an armored car, practically landing at their feet. Sally quickly picked it up, but not sure what to do with it, they took it home. There, she counted the money--fifty-thousand dollars.

Andy said, "We've got to give it back." Sally said, "Finders keepers." She put the money back in the bag and hid it in their attic.

The next day, two FBI men were canvassing the neighborhood looking for the money, and knocked on the door. "Pardon me, but did either of you find a bag that fell out of an armored car yesterday."

Sally said, "No." Andy said, "She's lying. She hid it up in the attic." Sally said, "Don't believe him, he's getting senile." The agents turn to Andy and began to question him. One says: "Tell us the story from the beginning." Andy said, "Well, when Sally and I were walking home from school yesterday . . . . " The first FBI guy turns to his partner and says, "We're outta here."

Joe took his wife to the doctor. The doc came out and said, "Frankly, I don't like the way your wife looks."

"I don't either," said Joe, "but she's good to the kids."

My memory's not as sharp as it used to be.

Also, my memory's not as sharp as it used to be.

Know how to prevent sagging?

Just eat till the wrinkles fill out.

YOU'RE GETTING OLDER IF YOU CAN REMEMBER....

Being sent to the drugstore to test vacuum tubes for the TV or radio.

When Kool-Aid was the only other drink for kids, other than milk & sodas.

When there were types of sneakers for boys.

When boys couldn't wear anything but leather shoes to school.

When it took five minutes for the TV to warm up.

When nearly everyone's parents smoked.

When all your friends got their hair cut at the kitchen table.

When nearly everyone's mom was at home when the kids got there.

When nobody owned a pure-bred dog.

When a dime was a decent allowance, & a quarter a huge bonus.

When you'd reach into a muddy gutter for a penny.

When girls neither dated nor kissed until late high school, if then.

When mom wore nylons that came in two pieces.

When all your teachers wore either neckties or had their hair done, everyday.

When Bible reading & prayer started school days.

When you got your windshield cleaned, oil checked, & gas pumped, without asking, for free, every time & you got trading stamps to boot.

When laundry detergent had free glasses, dishes or towels hidden inside the box.

When any parent could discipline any kid, or feed him, or use him to carry groceries, & nobody, not even the kid, thought a thing of it.

When it was considered a great privilege to be taken out to dinner at a real restaurant with your parents.

When they threatened to keep kids back a grade if they failed-& did.

When women were called, "Mrs. John Smith, instead of their own name.

When being sent to the principal's office was nothing compared to the fate that awaited a misbehaving student at home.

SUNRISE IN HEAVEN

I dreamed death came the other night
And heaven's gate swung open wide,
An angel with a halo bright
Ushered me inside.

And there! To my astonishment,
Stood folks I'd judged and labeled
As “quite unworthy” of little worth
And “spiritually disabled.”

Indignant words rose to my lips
But never were set free,
For every face showed stunned surprise-
Not one expected ME!

ABOUT YOUR AGE

Do you realize that the only time in our lives when we like to get old is when we're kids? If you're less than ten years old, you're so excited about aging that you think in fractions. Examples:

“How old are you?”

“I'm four and a half.”

You're never 36 and a half ....you're four and a half going on 5.

You get into your teens; now they can't hold you back.

You jump to the next number. "How old are you?" "I'm gonna be 16." You could be 12, but you're gonna be 16 eventually.

Then the great day of your life; you become 21. Even the words sound like a ceremony. You BECOME 21....Yes!!

Then you turn 30. What happened there? Makes you sound like bad milk. He TURNED; we had to throw him out. What's wrong?

What changed? You BECOME 21; you TURN 30.

Then you're PUSHING 40....stay over there. You REACH 50.

You BECOME 21; you TURN 30; You're PUSHING 40; you REACH 50-then you MAKE IT to 60.

By then you've built up so much speed, you HIT 70. You get into your 80's; you HIT lunch, you HIT 4:30.

And it doesn't end there....

Into the 90's, you start going backwards. "I was JUST 92."

Then a strange thing happens; if you make it over 100, you become a little kid again.. "I'm 100 and a half!!!"

Happy Aging!!

Getting old isn't so bad - when you consider the alternative.

When a man gets too old to set a bad example, he starts giving good advice.

Just remember this gals: The best years of your life are those you gave to the guy who made them the best years of your life.

OH MAN!

A man's life is full of trouble. He comes into the world without his consent and goes out usually against his will, and the trip between his coming and going is exceedingly rocky. The rule of contraries is one of the features of this journey.

When he is little, the big girls kiss him: but when he is big, only little girls kiss him. If he is poor, he's said to be a bad manager; if he's rich, they claim he's dishonest.

If he needs credit, he can't get it; if he's prosperous, everyone wants to do him a favor. If he's in politics, they say he takes graft; if he's not in politics, he's not patriotic. If he gives to charity, it's for show. If he doesn't, he's stingy.

If he's actively religious, some say he's a hypocrite; if he doesn't take a deep interest in religion, they call him a sinner. If he gives affection, he's a soft specimen. If he cares for nobody, they say he's cold-blooded.

If he dies young, there was a great future for him, if he lives to be old, he missed his calling.

If he saves money, he's a miser; if he spends it, he's a squanderer.

If he works very hard, they say he's crazy; if he doesn't work, he's a bum...so what's the use?

-- Anonymous

MY GET-UP AND GO--JUST GOT UP AND WENT

How do I know that my youth is all spent?
Well, my get-up-and-go just got up and went.
But in spite of it all I'm able to grin
When I think of where my get-up has been.
Old age is golden, I've heard it said;
But sometimes I wonder as I get into bed
My eyes on the table until I get up.
'Ere sleep dims my eyes I say to myself
Is there anything else I should lay on the shelf?
But I'm happy to say, as I close my door,
My friends are the same, perhaps even more.
When I was young, my slippers were red,
I could kick my heels right over my head.
When I grew older my slippers were blue

And I could dance the whole night
through.
Now, I'm old, my slippers are black
I walk to the corner--then I walk back.
The reason--I know--my youth is all spent
My get-up-and-go just got up and went.
But I really don't mind, when I think with
a grin,
Of all the grand places my get-up has
been.
Since I've retried from life's competition
I busy myself with complete competition.
I get up each morning, dust off my wits,
I pick up the paper and read the obits.
If my name is missing, I know I'm not
dead
So I eat a good breakfast--and go back to
bed.
--Author Unknown

CALLING ALL SHUT-INS

Oh, all you shut-ins, sick abed,
Or helpless in a chair,
Who fear your lives are not worthwhile
You have much time for prayer.

We who must spend our days in work
Wish for more time to pray;
For, oh so many need our prayers,
At home or far away.

The pastors, teachers, pupils, too,
And all who are distressed
By illness or by fears and cares
Can through your prayers be blest.

Say not there's nothing you can do
While you are lying there;
The great vocation can be yours
Of intercessory prayer.
--Gertrude E. Warchow

Passed years seem safe ones, vanquished ones, while the future lives in a cloud, formidable from a distance. The cloud clears as you enter it. I have learned this, but like everyone, I learned it late.

--Beryl Markha

DRINKING FROM THE SAUCER

I've never made a fortune,
And I'll never
Make one now.
But it really doesn't matter
Cause I am happy anyhow.
As I go along my journey
I'm reaping better
Than I've sowed.

I'm drinking
From the saucer
Cause my cup
Has overflowed.

I don't have a lot of riches
And sometimes
The going's tough
But I've got my kids
To love me so
I think I'm rich enough.
I'll just thank God
For the blessings
That His mercy
Has bestowed.
I'm drinking
From the saucer
Cause my cup
Has overflowed.

If you give me
Strength and courage
When the way grows steep
And rough,
I'll not ask
For other blessings since
I'm already blest enough.
May I never be too busy
To help another's load
Then I'll be drinking
From the saucer

Cause my cup
Has overflowed.
--Anonymous

THE EIGHT STAGES OF LIFE

Spills,
Drills,
Thrills,
Skills,
Bills,
Ills,
Pills,
And Wills.

MY BAGGY LONG UNDERWEAR

When I see in winter the legs so bare,
I remember my long baggy underwear;
For in spite of anything I would do,
That big, bulky wrinkle hung over my shoe.

I would try so hard to tuck them in tight,
And think the things would hold all right;
But in spite of all that I could do,
My underwear bulged over the top of my shoe.

I wound and I stretched them in firm at the heel
And drew them so tight I could almost

squeal;
But in school, in spite of all I'd do,
My long, baggy underwear bulged over my
shoe.

Young folks today should achieve great
things,
Rise to famed heights on glorious wings,
For they need not take time as I had to do,
To fret o'er long undies that bagged o'er my
shoe.
--Frances Brown

A young six year old boy was given a tape of *Joshua Fit the Battle of Jericho* for his birthday and a small make believe microphone. A few weeks later his grandmother heard him singing, "Joshua filled the bottle with Cherry Coke."

--Betty Gray, used by Permission

HOW THINGS CHANGE

Everything is farther away than it used to be. It is twice as far to the corner, and they have added a hill. I noticed I have given up running for the bus, it leaves faster than it used to. And it seems to me they are making stairs steeper than the old days.

Have you noticed the smaller print they are using in the newspaper? And there is no sense in asking people to read out loud -- every one speaks in such a low voice, I can hardly hear them.

The material in dresses is so skimpy now especially around the hips and waist. It is almost impossible to reach my shoelaces. Even people are changing. They are so much younger than they used to be when I was their age. On the other hand people my age are so much older than I am.

I ran into an old classmate the other day, and she had aged so much I didn't even recognize her.

I got to thinking about the poor thing while I was combing my hair this morning and in doing so I glanced at my reflection. You know they don't even make mirrors like they used to either.

--Author Unknown

You know you're getting old when you start riding a bike and your kids take the car!

HOW TO KNOW YOU ARE GROWING OLDER

Everything hurts and what doesn't hurt,
doesn't work.
The gleam in your eyes is from the sun
hitting your bifocals.
You feel like the night before, and you
haven't been anywhere.
Your little black book contains only
names ending in M.D.
You get winded playing chess.
Your children begin to look middle-aged.
You finally get to the top of the ladder,
and find it leaning against the wrong wall.
You join a health club and don't go.
You decide to procrastinate but then
never get around to it.
You're still chasing women, but can't
remember why.
Your mind makes contracts your body
can't meet.
You know all the answers, but nobody
asks you the questions.
You look forward to a dull evening.
You walk with your head held high, trying
to get used to your bifocals.
Your favorite part of the newspaper is 25
years ago today.
You turn out the light for economic rather
than romantic reasons.

You sit in a rocking chair and can't make it go.

Your knees buckle and your belt won't.

You regret all those mistakes resisting temptation.

You're 17 around the neck, 42 around the waist, and 96 around the golf course.

You stop looking forward to your next birthday.

After painting the town red, you have to take a long rest before, applying a second coat.

Dialing long distance wears you out.

You're startled the first time you are addressed as old timer.

You remember today, that yesterday was your wedding anniversary.

You just can't stand people who are intolerant.

The best part of your day is over when your alarm clock goes off.

You burn the midnight oil after 9 p.m.

Your back goes out more then you do.

A fortune-teller offers to read your face.

Your pacemaker makes the garage door go up when you watch a pretty girl go by.

The little gray-haired lady you help across the street is your wife.

You get exercise acting as a pallbearer for your friends who exercise.

You have too much room in the house and not enough in the medicine cabinet.
You sink your teeth into a steak and they stay there.

I'm glad the Lord planned for the young people to have the babies. If we older people had them and laid them down, we'd forget where we put them.

CLIMB THE WALLS

"Oh, I sure am happy to see you," the little boy said to his grandmother on his mother's side. "Now maybe daddy will do the trick he has been promising us."

The grandmother was curious. "What trick is that?" she asked.

"I heard him tell mommy that he would climb the walls if you came to visit," the little boy answered.

Behind every successful man there is very surprised mother-in-law.

If at first you don't succeed, try doing it the way she told you to.

YOU'RE NOT A KID ANYMORE WHEN....

You're asleep, but others worry that you're dead.

You quit trying to hold your stomach in, no matter who walks into the room.

You buy a compass for the dash of your car.

You are proud of your lawn mower.

Your best friend is dating someone half his age. . . and isn't breaking any laws.

You call Olin Mills before they call you.

Your arms are almost too short to read the newspaper.

You sing along with the elevator music.

You would rather go to work than stay home sick.

You constantly talk about the price of gasoline.

You enjoy hearing about other people's operations.

You make an appointment to see the dentist.

You no longer think of speed limits as a challenge.

Your Neighbors borrow your tools.

Your friends call at 9 p.m. and ask, "Did I wake you?"

You have a dream about prunes.

You answer a question with, "Because I said so!"
You send money to PBS.
You still buy records, and you think a CD is a certificate of deposit.
Your tie doesn't come anywhere near the top of your pants.
You take a metal detector to the beach.
You wear black socks with sandals.
You know what the word 'equity' means.
You can't remember the last time you lay on the floor to watch television.
You talk about "good grass," and you're referring to someone's lawn.
You get into a heated argument about pension plans.
You got cable for the weather channel.
You can go bowling without drinking.
You have a party, and the neighbors don't even realize it.

THE WATER PISTOL

When my three-year-old son opened the birthday gift from his grandmother, he discovered a water pistol... he squealed with delight and headed for the nearest sink.

I was not so pleased. I turned to mom and said, "I'm surprised at you. Don't you remember how we used to drive you crazy with water guns?"

Mom smiled and then replied..... "I remember!!"

Just about the time you think you can make ends meet, somebody moves the ends.

Husbands: a minority in a group of two.

"FLOUR SACK UNDERWEAR"

When I was a maiden fair,
Momma made our underwear.
With five tots and Pa's poor pay,
How could she buy lingerie?

Monograms and fancy stitches,
Were not on our flour sack britches.
Panty waists that stood the test,
With Gold Medal on the chest.

Little pants the best of all,
With scenes that I can still recall.
Harvesters were gleaning wheat,
Right across the little seat.

Tougher than a grizzly bear,
Was our flour sack underwear.
Plain or fancy, 3 feet wide,
Stronger than a hippo's hide.

Through the years each Jack and Jill

Wore this garb against their will.
Waste not, want not, we soon learned,
And a penny saved is a penny earned.

Bedspreads, curtains, tea towels and
Tablecloths to name a few.
But the best beyond compare,
Was always that flour sack underwear.
--Author Unknown

THE PERKS OF BEING OVER 60

People no longer view you as a hypochondriac.
Your eyes won't get much worse.
Things you buy now won't wear out.
Men can quit holding in their stomachs when a lady walks into the room.
Men have more hair on their ears than on their heads.
In a hostage situation, you are likely to be released first.
There's nothing left to learn the hard way.
Your joints are more accurate than the National Weather Service.
Your back goes out more than you do.
Your conversation with other people is a comparison of aches, pains, operations and pills.
No one expects you to run into a burning building.

You can eat dinner at 4 PM.
You got cable for the weather channel.
Your supply of brain cells is finally down to a manageable size.
Your investment in health insurance is finally beginning to pay off.
Kidnappers are not very interested in you.
Your secrets are safe with your friends because they can't remember them either.
You consider coffee one of the most important things in life.

BATTLE HYMN OF AGING

We reach the age of 65 - our golden years are here.
They tell us that the age begins - a happy new career.
For now our Uncle Sam becomes - our permanent cashier as we go marching on.

Our Social Security from Baltimore is sent.
We buy a little bit of food - and maybe pay the rent.
And after that, we're stony broke - and left without a cent, but we go bravely on.

And as for checks from Medicare - will someone tell us how?
They always find some doctor bills - they sadly disallow?

And dental cost as well we know they wholly disallow, but we go bravely on.

And first of all, let's thank the Lord that we are still alive,
The dreams we have may still come true when we are ninety-five,
So, please dear Lord, give us the strength our troubles to survive, as we go bravely on.

Glory, Glory, Hallelujah
Glory, Glory, Hallelujah
Glory, Glory, Hallelujah
As we go bravely on.

After putting her grandchildren to bed, a grandmother changed into old slacks and a droopy blouse and proceeded to wash her hair. As she heard the children getting more and more rambunctious, her patience grew thin. Finally, the threw a towel around her head and stormed into their room, putting them back to bed with stern warnings. As she left the room, she heard the three-year-old say with a trembling voice, "Who was THAT?"

My grandson was visiting one day when he asked, "Grandpa, do you know how you and God are alike?" I mentally polished my halo and said, "No, how are we alike?" "You're both old," he replied.

I didn't know if my granddaughter had learned her colors yet, so I decided to test her. I would point out something and ask what color it was. She would tell me and was always correct. It was fun for me, so I continued. At last, she headed for the door, saying, "Grandma, I think you should try to figure out some of these yourself!"

When my grandson and I entered our vacation cabin, we kept the lights off until we were inside to keep from attracting pesky insects. Still, a few fireflies followed us in. Noticing them before I did, my grandson whispered, "It's no use Grandpa. Now the mosquitoes are coming after us with flashlights."

AN OLD MAN AND THE LITTLE BOY

Said the little boy,
"Sometimes I drop my spoon".
Said the little old man,
"And I do that, too."

The little boy whispered,
"I wet my pants."
"I do that, too"

Laughed the little old man.

Said the little boy,
"I often cry."
The old man nodded,
"So do I."

"But worst of all," said the boy, "it seems
Grownups don't pay attention to me."
And he felt the warmth of a wrinkled old
    hand,
"I know what you mean,"
Said the little old man.

As she watched her grandmother embroider an intricate quilt, our four-year-old granddaughter hopefully queried, "When I get a little older, will you teach me how to color with thread?"

--T. LaMance

A HUSBAND'S CHECKUP

A woman accompanied her husband to the doctor's office. After his checkup, the doctor called the wife into his office alone.

He said, "Your husband is suffering from a very severe disease, combined with horrible stress. If you don't do the following, your husband will surely die."

"Each morning, fix him a healthy breakfast. Be pleasant, and make sure he is in a good mood. For lunch make him a nutritious meal. For dinner prepare an especially nice meal for him. Don't burden him with chores, as he probably had a hard day. Don't discuss your problems with him, it will only make his stress worse. And most importantly, satisfy his every whim. If you can do this for the next 10 months to a year, I think your husband will regain his health completely."

On the way home, the husband asked his wife, "What did the doctor say?"

"You're going to die," she replied.

Amazed at seeing her mother turn on the car's windshield washer spray, our three-year-old grand-daughter wanted to know, "Can you make it snow too?"

RETIREMENT DEFINITIONS

Sixty-five is the age when one acquires sufficient experience to lose his job.

There are a lot of books telling you how to manage when you retire. What most people want is one that will tell them how to manage in the meantime.

Retirement can be a great joy if you can figure how to spend time without spending money.

Forty years ago when a fellow said something about retiring, he was talking about going to bed.

"Retirement Security" is making sure all the doors are locked before you go to bed.

The key to happy retirement is to have enough money to live on, but not enough to worry about.

One wife's definition of retirement: "Twice as much husband, and half as much income."

Mandatory retirement is another form of compulsory poverty.

Retirement has cured many a business man's ulcers—and given them to his wife.

COUNT YOUR BLESSINGS

If your arteries have hardened and arthritis
slows your gait,
If your tired blood is stubborn, not inclined to
circulate;
If your aerobic days are over and you cannot
do the "twist",
If your time is spent in brooding o'er the many
things you've missed;
If you're constantly complaining on your
rocker or your couch,
If you're ornery and cranky and becoming

quite a grouch;
Well, if this is your condition and you get no sympathy,
Then it's time you started trying a new kind of therapy.

Though you have your share of trouble, think of others with more pain,
Like that fellow in his wheelchair who will never walk again.
Take time to write a letter and while the pen is in your palm,
Thank the good Lord up above you for the use of that right arm.
Try relaxing in the sunshine, note each flower, bird and tree,
Then appreciate your eyesight - there are many who can't see.
When you tune in television and each sound is loud and clear,
Just think of those who'd give a lot if only they could hear.
Yes, I've practiced what I'm preaching and I've learned there's joy to reap,
If you stop and count your blessings and just "think before you weep."

--Author Unknown

An elderly, wealthy woman in Florida was

boring fellow beachcombers as she bragged on and on about her two remarkable grandchildren.

Unable to stand it any longer, a fellow sunbather interrupted her.

"Tell me, how old are your grandsons?"

The grandmother gave a grateful smile and replied, "The doctor is four and the lawyer is six..."

I AIN'T DEAD YET!

My hair is white and I'm almost blind,
The days of my youth are far behind.
My neck is stiff and I can't turn my head,
Can't hear one-half of what's being said,
My legs are wobbly, can hardly walk,
But, glory be, I can surely talk.
And this is the message I want you to get--
I'm still a kickin' and I ain't dead yet.

My joints are still, won't move in their
    sockets
And nary a dime is left in my pockets.
So maybe you think I'm a total wreck,
To tell you the truth, I do look like heck!
But still I do have a lot of fun,
And my heart with joy is overrun.
I've lots of friends, so kind and so sweet,
And still more that I'll never meet.

Oh this is a wonderful world of ours,
Shade and sunshine and beautiful flowers.
So you can take it from me, you bet!
I'm glad I'm livin' and I ain't dead yet.
I've got corns on my feet and ingrown nails,
And do they hurt? Here plain language fails.
To tell you my troubles would take too long,
And if I tried you'd surely give me the gong.

I go to church and Sunday school
For I love the story that is ever new,
And when I reach the end of my row,
I hope to the lovely home I'll go.
And then when I leave this house of clay,
If you listen quite closely I'm quite apt to say,
"Well, folks, I've left you, but don't you forget
I've just passed on and I ain't dead yet."
–Grandma Josie

During my brother's wedding, my mother had managed to keep from crying -- until she glanced at my grandparents. My grandmother had reached over to my grandfather's wheelchair and gently touched his hand. That was all it took to start my mother's tears flowing. After the wedding, Mom went over to my grandmother and told her how that tender gesture triggered her outburst. "Well, I'm sorry to ruin your moment," Grandmother replied.

"But I was just checking to see if he was awake."

Wisdom comes with age, but it doesn't do anybody much good, since humility tends to set in about the same time.

Streams of water become crooked from taking the path of least resistance
So do people.

"THE GOOD OLD DAYS! "

Mama's mama, on a winter's day,
Milked the cows and fed them hay,
Slopped the hogs, saddled the mule,
And got the children off to school.

Swept the parlor, made the bed,
Baked a dozen loaves of bread,
Split some firewood and lugged it in,
Enough to fill the kitchen bin.

Cleaned the lamps and put in oil,
Stewed some apples she thought might spoil,
Churned the butter, baked a cake,
Then exclaimed, "For mercy's sake!"

"The calves have got out of the pen!"
Went out and chased them in again.
Gathered the eggs and locked the stable,
Returned to the house and set the table.

Cooked a supper that was delicious,
And afterwards washed all the dishes,
Fed the cat, sprinkled the clothes,
Mended a basket full of hose.

Then opened the organ and began to play
"When you come to the end of a perfect day."

MY 90TH BIRTHDAY WISH

Today, dear Lord, I'm 90 and so much I haven't done,
I hope, dear Lord, You'll let me live until I'm 91.

But then if I haven't finished all that I would do,
Would you let me stay awhile, until I'm 92?

So many places I want to go and so very much to see,
Do you think you could manage to make it 93?

The world is changing very fast, there is
so much in store
So if it's all the same to You, I'd like to live
'till I'm 94.

And if by then I'm still alive,
I'd love to stay 'til maybe 95.

Bigger planes will fly and rockets fixed,
So I'd really like to stick around and see
what happens if I'm 96.

I know dear Lord, it's much to ask, I know
its nice in heaven,
But I'd really like to stay until I'm 97.

I know by then I won't be very fast and
sometimes very late,
But it would be my pleasure to be around
at 98.

I will have seen so many things and had a
wonderful time,
So I'm sure I'll be willing to leave at 99.

99's OK but listen if You would - there's
still a lot that I might miss,
So if the body's OK and I'm not a bore
what's wrong with staying until
I'm 104!!

THE SOCK AND THE WASHER

It's a repeat occurrence-
One that often comes about.
Two socks go in my washer,
And only one comes out;
Can this puzzle be explained?
What happens to the one?
Do washers go from "Wash" to "Rinse"
To "Sock Oblivion"?
If you have solved the problem,
I'd really like to know,
So I won't forever wonder
Where my missing socks go.
--Juliana Lewis

THINK ABOUT IT

Have you ever been unfairly criticized?
Falsely judged? Perhaps gossiped about?
If so, this thought may interest you....

When some fellow yields to temptation
And breaks a conventional law,
We look for no good in his makeup
But God! How we look for a flaw!

No one will ask, "How tempted?"
Nor allow for the battle he's fought;
His name becomes food for the jackals;
For us who have never been caught.

"He has sinned!" we shout from the
housetops.
We forget the time he has won.
"Come, gaze on the sinner!" We thunder,
"And by his example he taught
That his footsteps lead to destruction,"
Cry we who have never been caught.

I'm a sinner, O Lord, and I know it,
I'm weak, I blunder, I fail
I'm tossed on life's stormy ocean
Like ships embroiled in a gale.

I'm willing to trust in Thy mercy
To keep the commandments Thou has
taught,
But deliver me, Lord, from the judgment
Of those who have never been caught.

CAN'T REMEMBER

When you're on in years, it seems a shame
You have such a hard time remembering a
name.
Your memory flees when you need it most
It just seems to go and give up the ghost.
When you fill out a form, it's really a
bummer.
You can't remember your telephone
number.

There are even times it seems of late
I can't remember in what restaurant I ate.
Some times my memory really goes to pot
I can't find my car in the parking lot.
When someone asks me what book I have
read.
The title just slips right out of my head.

Once when dear hubby was trying to be
funny.
Said, "Gee, you never forget when I owe you
money
Or I never notice you having any distress
Knowing when and where there's a sale on
a dress"
"That's a cheap shot," I reply in dismay.
"Just wait till it happens to you someday."

Now it didn't take long to hubby's chagrin
The same thing started happening to him.
I sent him shopping while I stayed home
He came back empty handed and started to
moan
"I forgot my wallet," he sheepishly said
His face turned a lovely shade of red.

I started to smile and then to tease
When hubby couldn't find his keys.
We looked near and we searched far
And discovered he'd left them in the car.

There's much more to write, as I sit in my
den
But golly--I forgot where I left my pen.

At my father-in-law's 60th Class Reunion Committee meeting, the question came up as to what kind of awards to give out. My father-in-law, who had suffered numerous health problems recently, suggested an award for the person with the most prescriptions.

--Carole Christman Koch

A MARRIAGE PROPOSAL

Bill and Joe were residents at the retirement center. Joe was dating Mary, also a resident. One morning, Joe confided in Bill, "Last night I asked Mary to marry me, and I cannot remember what she said."

Bill said, "Go to the house phone and call her and ask her what her answer was."

So Joe calls her and when she answered, he said, "Mary, this is Joe. I'm embarrassed to call, but last night I asked you to marry me and I can't remember what you said."

Mary exclaimed, "Oh, Joe. I'm so glad you called, I told you 'yes' but I'd forgotten who it was who asked me!"

EVERYONE KNOWS NOW

A grandmother and her young grandson—who was in the shopping cart, were shopping at Wal-Mart. He spelled everything he passed. As they passed the panty hose display in a loud voice he spelled the letters. "Q U E E N S I Z E."

"Grand mother" he shouted, "do you know you are the same size as my bed?"

--Betty Gray, used by Permission

OLD FOLKS ARE VALUABLE

Remember Old Folks are worth a fortune, with silver in their hair, gold in their teeth, stones in their kidneys, lead in their feet, rust in their joints magnesium in their pills, iron in their blood, and gas in their stomachs.

I have become a little older since I saw you last and a few changes have come into my life since then.

Frankly I have become quite a frivolous old gal. I am seeing five gentlemen every day. As soon as I wake up, Will Power gets me out of bed. Then I go to see John. Then Charlie Horse comes along, and when he is here he takes a lot of my time and attention. When he leaves, Arthur Ritis shows up and stays the rest of the day. He doesn't like to stay in one place very long, so he takes me from joint to joint. After such a busy day I'm really tired and glad to go to bed with Ben Gay. What a life!

P.S. The preacher came to call the other day. He said at my age I should be thinking about the hereafter. I told him, "Oh, I do all the time. No matter where I am, in the parlor, upstairs, in the kitchen or down in the basement, I ask myself, "Now... what am I here after???"

I used to buy head and shoulders and now I buy mop and glo.

--Betty Gray, used by Permission

THE GOLDEN AGE

Nobody cares what an old woman wears:
Nobody notices--nobody cares,
And so I go home and do as I please,
With my hair yanked back--and my soul at
ease.

But once in awhile, the old fires burn,
And to ribbons and laces and flowers I turn,
And with ear rings abob and hair gently
curled,
I go out and look at the wide, wide world.

Nobody notices and nobody cares:

An old woman's an old woman, whatever she wears
And so--I go home and do as I please,
With my hair yanked back and my soul at ease.

THE SEVEN AGES OF MAN

20 is when you want to wake up employed.
30 is when you want to wake up married.
40 is when you want to wake up successful.
50 is when you want to wake up rich.
60 is when you want to wake up contented.
70 is when you want to wake up healthy.
80 is when you want to wake up.

THE NICE THING ABOUT GRANDPARENTS IS...

They like to hold you in their laps.
They don't get mad when you don't eat your vegetables.
They boost your confidence.
They like kids, and dogs, and cats.
They really know how to tuck you in at night.
They're not in such a hurry.
They listen to funny music.
They have the nicest smelling house.
They always buy what you're selling.
They don't mind when you make noise.

They help with homework...They don't always know the answers, but they try.
They never say "Hurry up."
They give good presents for your birthday.
They are the only grown-ups who have the time.
They like to go to the park--they don't go on the monkey bars, though.
They think you're the smartest, cutest kid on earth.
They give you money and never say it has to be saved.
They like it when you sleep at their house.
They understand you when you cry.
They take you places in their RV.
They know how to explain things to Mom and Dad.
They show your picture to everyone.
They never put you on hold when they get a call- waiting signal.
They listen to what you say.
They have some weird old toys.
They don't skip parts of a story or mind if it is the same story over again.
They say they knew Mom and Dad when they were kids.

--Source Unknown

THIS CHANGING WORLD

When Grandma came to visit us,
We gathered 'round her chair,
And while she told us of "old times",
We stroked her silvery hair.
We knew that spicy gingerbread,
Small pies and cherry tarts,
And chicken dumplings, light as air,
Would soon delight out hearts.

My children's Grandma breezes in
With steps light as a girl,
With tinted lips and fingernails,
And soft hair all a-curl.
In gym suit she defies her age:
Today, young daughter said:
"To keep her arteries O.K.
Grandma stands on her head."

WHEN I'M AN OLD LADY

When I'm an old lady, I'll live with my kids,
And make their life happy and filled with such fun.
I want to pay back all the joy they've provided,
Returning each deed. Oh they'll be so excited.

When I'm an old lady and live with my kids.
I'll write on the wall with red, white, and blue
And bounce on the furniture wearing my shoes.

I'll drink from the carton and then leave it out.
I'll stuff all the toilets and oh, they'll shout.

When I'm an old lady and live with my kids,
When they're on the phone and just out of reach,
I'll get into things like sugar and bleach.

Oh, they'll snap their fingers and then shake their heads
And when that is done, I'll hide under the bed.

When I'm an old lady and live with my kids,
When they cook dinner and call me to meals,
I'll not eat my green beans or salads congealed.

I'll gag on my okra, spill milk on the table,

And when they get angry, run fast as I'm able.

When I'm an old lady and live with my kids.
I'll sit close to the TV, through the channels I'll click.
I'll cross both my eyes to see if they stick.

I'll take off my socks and throw one away.
And I'll lay back and sigh, and thank God in prayer,
And then close my eyes and my kids will look down,
With a smile slowly creeping and say with a groan,
"She's so sweet when she's sleeping."
When I'm an old lady and live with my kids.

--Clipped

Two elderly ladies were enjoying the sunshine on a park bench in Miami.

They had been meeting in that park every sunny day for 12 years, chatting and enjoying each other's friendship.

One day, one of the ladies turned to the other and said, "Please don't be angry with me, dear, but I am embarrassed. After all these years ... What is your name? I am trying to remember, but I just can't."

The friend stared at her, looking very distressed. She said nothing for two full minutes, and finally, with tearful eyes said, "How soon do you have to know?"

OLD GEEZERS

"Old Geezers" are easy to spot; this is slang for an old man. At sporting events, during the playing of the National Anthem, they hold their caps over their hearts and sing without embarrassment.

"Old Geezers" know the words and believe in them. They remember World War 1, the Depression, World War 2, Pearl Harbor, Guadalcanal, Normandy, and Hitler. They remember the Atomic Age, the Korean War, The Cold War, the Jet Age and the Moon Landing, not to mention Vietnam.

"Old Geezers" get embarrassed if someone curses in front of women and children and they don't like violence and filth on TV or in movies or in emails. "Old Geezers" have moral courage.

"Old Geezers" seldom brag, unless it is about their grandchildren.

It's the "Old Geezers" who know our great country is protected, not by politicians, but by the young men and women in the military, voluntarily serving our country.

If you bump into an "Old Geezer" on the sidewalk, he'll apologize, pass an "Old Geezer" on the street, he'll nod, or tip his cap to a lady.

"Old Geezers" trust strangers and are courtly to women. They hold the door for the next person and always when walking, make sure the lady is on the inside for protection.

This country need "Old Geezers" with their decent values.

We need them more than ever.

Thank God for "Old Geezers!"

--Author Unknown

BEATITUDES FOR FRIENDS OF THE AGED

Blessed are they who understand that age doesn't make me less a man.

Blessed are they who expect me to be the very best that I can be.

Blessed are they who seem to know I have something left that still can grow.

Blessed are they who take the time to learn what I was in my prime.

Blessed are they who know that I am still somebody until I die.

Blessed are they who know my needs and the things on which my ego feeds.

Blessed are they who make it known I can make decisions on my own.

Blessed are they who hear what I say and know that I still am seeking a way

To be <u>somebody</u> to have <u>my</u> day before this world's pleasures have faded away.

--Martin Smith

The young man who thought the world owed him a living is now the old man who is blaming the world for his failure.

Any man who thinks he is more intelligent than his wife is married to a really smart lady.

Be sure your footprints on the sand of time leave more than a big heel.

SLOW ME DOWN LORD

Slow me down Lord!
    Ease the pounding of my heart
    By the quieting of my mind.
Steady my harried pace
    With a vision of the eternal reach of time.
Give me,
    Amidst the confusions of my day,
    The calmness of the everlasting hills.
Break the tensions of my nerves
    With the soothing music of the singing streams

That live in my memory.
Help me know
The magical restoring power of sleep.
Teach me the art
Of taking minute vacations of slowing down
to look at a flower;
to chat with an old friend or make a new one;
to pat a stray dog;
to watch a spider build a web;
to smile at a child;
or to read a few lines from a good book.
Remind me each day
That the race is not always to the swift;
That there is more to life than increasing its speed.
Let me look upward
Into the branches of the towering oak
And know that it grew slowly and well.
Slow me down, Lord,
And inspire me to send my roots deep
into the soil of life's enduring values
That I may grow toward the stars
Of my greater destiny.
--Wilfred A. Peterson

A LITTLE MIXED UP

Just a line to say I'm living,

That I'm not among the dead;
Though I'm getting more forgetful,
And more mixed up in the head.
For, sometimes, I can't remember,
When I stand at foot of stair,
If I must go up for something,
Or I've just come down from there.
And before the frig' so often,
My poor mind is filled with doubt,
Have I just put food away, or
Have I come to take some out.
And there's times when it is dark out,
With my night cap on my head,
I don't know if I'm retiring,
Or just getting out of bed.
So, if it's my turn to write you,
There's no need in getting sore,
I may think that I have written,
And don't want to be a bore.
So, remember---I do love you,
And I wish, that you were here;
But now, it's nearly mail time,
So I must day, "Goodbye, dear."
There I stood beside the mailbox,
With a face so very red,
Instead of mailing you my letter,
I had opened it instead!

GO ON WITH YOUR KNITTIN'

When the folks next to you act like those in

the zoo
A grumblin', growlin' and spitin'
It's a pretty good plan
To be calm as you can
And do something useful--like knittin'.

When a gossipin' Susan with poison barbed tongue
Comes into the room where you're sittin'
And starts to defame
Some neighbor's good name
Count your stitches out loud and keep knittn'.

When there's been a slight misunderstanding at church
And others hint broadly of quittin'
Why the very best thing
You can do is to sing
And stay at your post and keep knittin'.

When Satan moves in with his cohorts of sin
Say "You'll never find me submittin'
You irk me I find
So get thee behind
And please don't disturb me--I'm knittin'."

In the middle of problems the big ones and small
It's always proper and fittin'

To trust and to pray
Till the Lord shows the way
And go right ahead with your knittin'.
--Author Unknown

INNER PEACE

If you can start the day without caffeine,
If you can always be cheerful, ignoring aches and pains,
If you can resist complaining and boring people with your troubles,
If you can eat the same food every day and be grateful for it,
If you can understand when your loved ones are too busy to give you any time,
If you can take criticism and blame without resentment,
If you can conquer tension without medical help,
If you can relax without liquor,
If you can sleep without the aid of drugs,
Then You Are Probably The Family Dog!

PRAYER FOR THE AGED

"Lord, thou knowest better than I know myself that I am growing older and will someday be old.
"Keep me from getting talkative, and particularly from the fatal habit of thinking

I must say something on every occasion.
"Release me from craving to try to straighten out everybody's affairs.
"Keep my mind free from the recital of endless details--give me wings to get to the point.
"I ask for grace enough to listen to the tales of others' pains. Help me to endure them with patience.
"But seal my lips on my own aches and pains--they are increasing and my love of rehearsing them is becoming sweeter as the years go by.
"Teach me that glorious lesson that occasionally it is possible that I may be mistaken.
"Keep me reasonably sweet; I do not want to be saint --some of them are so hard to live with--but a sour old person is one of the crowning works of the devil.
"Make me thoughtful, but not moody; helpful, but not bossy.
With my vast store of wisdom, it seems a pity not to use it all, but thou knowest, Lord, that I want a few friends at the end.
"Help me to extract all possible fun out of life. There are so many funny things around us and I don't want to miss any of them.
In Jesus Name I pray-------AMEN."

OTHER BOOKS BY GLEN WHEELER

Bedpan Devotions - *Reflections on Recovering from an Extended Illness.*

Excellent counsel for those with long term home confinement, cancer, heart problems, broken bones, and similar illnesses.

Written while recovering from a broken hip, the chapters deal with the various emotions experienced thru a long illness – loneliness, fear, bills, blood draws, visitors, faith and prayers.

Nineteen chapters of helpful, personal, and at times humorous reading.

Available from the Author, Amazon, Barnes and Noble Bookstores, Koinonia Associates and local bookstores. Price:$12.95per copy. P/H and tax included. Published 2010.

Widowers Hurt, Too

After thirty-three years of a blessed marriage, Mr. Wheeler became a widower in 1981. He discovered that support materials to help men through the several adjustments are very few.

In this book, he outlines the many challenges, how he faced them and suggestions for the reader to consider. Some of the chapters are: "The Silence of the Night", "How do I Change the Sweeper Bag?", "One Check, Please.", "Good Night, See You in the Morning.", "Dare I Think of Remarriage?" and "Attending Church Alone." Ten additional subjects are discussed in the book.

Widows will benefit from the book, even though the title says, "Widowers."

Available from the Author, Amazon, Barnes and Noble Bookstores, Koinonia Associates and local bookstores. Price$12.95per copy. Published 2008 Reprinted 2009.

AUTHOR'S ADDRESS
Mr. Glen Wheeler
165 Highbluffs Blvd. # 413
Columbus, OH 43235

Email: gvwheeler@juno.com
Web: www.gvwheeler.com

KOINONIA ASSOCIATES ADDRESS
7809 Timber Glow Trail
Knoxville, TN 37938
PublishwithKA.com